'This book touches a critical nerve. The authors take an intelligent and pragmatic look at the issues. I applaud them on tackling this sweeping and all-important topic.'
Brian Bennett, *President Culinary Software Services, Inc. Boulder, CO, USA*

'The authors argue with clarity of thought and a strong conviction, that building and keeping trust lies at the heart of all successful organisations, irrespective of industry and culture, and that without it both organisations and leaders will ultimately fail. If any book can make a leader sit up and take notice of this essential truth, this is the one!'
Rosemarie Wallace, *Regional Managing Director, Asia, Reader's Digest*

'Trust: a precious commodity; occurs naturally but easily broken; can be made from a strong solution of openness and integrity; shines in the dark and releases disproportionate amounts of energy, innovation and creativity; an essential ingredient for satisfaction and achievement. This book shows you how to understand and develop this rare and wonderful gift.'
John Harris, *former CEO of Calor Group*

'Speed, greed and expediency drive people and organizations to moral (and often financial) bankruptcy. Authenticity and respect cultivate trust, nurturing the tensions and lubricating the frictions of imperfect human behaviour in contemporary organizations. Sally Bibb and Jeremy Kourdi provide a clear and understandable range of supportive, practical ways to engender respect, authenticity and most of all renewed trust in contemporary organizations. This timely book is an insightful reminder of alternatives to the otherwise depressing stories of too many organizations in trouble.'
John Hofmeister, *Director Human Resources, Royal Dutch/Shell Group of Companies*

TRUST MATTERS

Trust Matters

For Organisational and Personal Success

Sally Bibb and Jeremy Kourdi

palgrave
macmillan

First published 2004 by
PALGRAVE MACMILLAN
Houndmills, Basingstoke, Hampshire RG21 6XS and
175 Fifth Avenue, New York, N.Y. 10010
Companies and representatives throughout the world

PALGRAVE MACMILLAN is the global academic imprint of the Palgrave Macmillan division of St. Martin's Press, LLC and of Palgrave Macmillan Ltd. Macmillan® is a registered trademark in the United States, United Kingdom and other countries. Palgrave is a registered trademark in the European Union and other countries.

ISBN 1–4039–3253–0

This book is printed on paper suitable for recycling and made from fully managed and sustained forest sources.

A catalogue record for this book is available from the British Library.

A catalog record for this book is available from the Library of Congress.

10 9 8 7 6 5 4 3 2 1
13 12 11 10 09 08 07 06 05 04

Printed and bound in Great Britain by
Creative Print & Design (Wales) Ebbw Vale

For Eric Bibb, who taught me about integrity and trust.

(Sally Bibb)

Contents

List of figures and tables

Preface

Everyone we approached to talk to about this book had something to say. When we told them we were writing a book about trust in organisations, an alarming number said 'don't you mean the lack of it?'

This response is hardly surprising when you consider that in recent years we have witnessed the breakdown of trust in some spectacular ways. We have seen the damage that can be done when trust breaks down in governments and corporations. Trust has always been important. It is a shame that it has taken such crises for us to realise this.

Trust is certainly a topic that gets people energised, no matter where in the world they are. Despite this, it is rarely the subject of conversation inside organisations. This is surprising, as trust is the foundation for all types of relationship, business and personal. Trust leads to employee commitment and motivation. It allows people to take risks, try new things and so encourages innovation. It increases customer loyalty because people would rather buy from companies they trust. Ultimately, it is central to success – whether that is the commercial success of a business, the electoral success of a political party, or the personal success of someone working effectively with others to achieve a goal.

Most organisations have not yet realised that developing trust is potentially a powerful source of competitive advantage. Consultants are not yet selling products and services that increase the trust quotient of your company, accelerate customer loyalty and give you the real answer to motivating your staff.

> **Most organisations have not yet realised that developing trust is a powerful source of competitive advantage.**

The number of books published on a particular management issue is usually a measure of one of several phenomena. It could be an indication of the perceived importance of the subject, as is the case with economic value added (EVA) for example. It is sometimes the result of a fear of getting it wrong; for example, there are many books about mergers and acquisitions and corporate governance. It can also be due to the extent to which managers feel they should be keeping up to date; leadership – especially transformational leadership – books fit this category. There are hundreds of such subjects that have become management fads, coming and going and often reinventing themselves several times. You only have to read the newspapers today to realise that politicians, corporate leaders and mighty PR people are getting very worried and giving serious consideration to how they rebuild trust.

They do indeed have a tough job. Creating trust is difficult enough. Rebuilding it when it has been lost is a task that takes a huge amount of commitment, as well as a great deal of skill and a rare understanding of the issues. Trust can be tough to define, complex to understand and hard to achieve, but the payoffs are exceptional.

Trust is too serious, significant and perennial to be viewed as a 'fad' or simple passing issue. It is central to individual and organisational success, yet for all its importance there is relatively little discussion of how we can build and develop trust. This book fills a gap in the market.

We do not promise easy, quick-fix solutions, but we raise questions that will put a glint in the eye of your customers and staff, and which all but the boldest manager might prefer to ignore. We show how successful organisations develop trust and what the key ingredients are. We set out to unravel the complexity, examine the issues and provide the ideas and experiences of people who have built high-trust organisations. The result is a roadmap to developing trust, and we hope you enjoy the journey.

In the text we sometimes say 'I'. This refers to Sally Bibb unless stated otherwise.

The contract

And in the end we follow them –
not because we are paid,
not because we might see some advantage,
not because of the things they have accomplished,
not even because of the dreams they dream,
but simply because of who they are:
the man, the woman, the leader, the boss,
standing up there when the waves hit the rock,
passing out faith and confidence like life jackets,
knowing the currents, holding the doubts,
imagining the delights and terrors of every landfall;
captain, pirate, and parent by turns,
the bearer of our countless hopes and expectations.
We give them our trust. We give them our effort.
What we ask in return is that they stay true.

William Ayot

Acknowledgements

Much of what I have learned has been from others and I am very lucky to know many wise and inspirational people; some I knew already, others I met in the course of writing this book.

A large number of people have contributed directly or indirectly to this project. I would especially like to thank the following for their support, generosity and challenge: Javier Bajer, Mary Clarke, Elaine Cronk, Susan Debnam, Gerard Fairtlough, Arie De Geus, Barbara Heinzen, Anna Phillips, Christie Rainbird, Kate Saunders and Vicky Vaughan.

I would also like to thank everyone that I have had a conversation with about this book. And there have been many such poor souls! Thanks too to all the contributors and to my colleagues and friends who, over the years, have provided me with many opportunities to learn about trust.

This book would not have been written without the support and commitment of Jeremy Kourdi. He is the most encouraging and patient of writing partners.

Finally, I thank my family, especially my parents, for their endless support, encouragement and enthusiasm about this and every other project I have ever undertaken.

Sally Bibb

Trust is an issue that is too often taken for granted. In my case, it took the wisdom of a talented senior executive and friend to highlight the power of trust in organisations, and how much greater levels of trust are needed in relationships. Sally Bibb's enthusiasm, insight and uncommon common sense ensured that this was always a stimulating project and pleasure to write.

Thanks must also go to Stephen Rutt and his team at Palgrave Macmillan. Their professionalism, support and commitment have been outstanding. Karen McCarthy and Steve Broomfield have given their time and expertise, and this is much appreciated. Kim Warren, Philippa Dickenson, Daniel Franklin and Steve Barrow have also provided valuable insights and comments about a topic in which they naturally excel.

Finally, my gratitude goes to my wife Julie, my son Thomas and my daughter Louise, who have provided constant support and encouragement as well as thought-provoking opinions and the inspiration to write.

Jeremy Kourdi

1 Building bridges or building walls?

Albert Einstein once said that the most important question human beings can ask themselves is whether the world is a friendly place or an unfriendly place, for their answer to that question determines whether they live their life building bridges or building walls.

In this chapter, we ask why, when trust has never been more relevant to our lives, it remains such a neglected issue. We ask what trust is and examine its relevance today.

CHANGING THE RULES OF ENGAGEMENT

Relationships and work would be so much more rewarding if we were better able to trust and be trusted. Not only that, but we could be more successful. Consider how it would be if we were able to change the rules of engagement so that our default position in relating to others was trust, instead of wariness, caution and circumspection.

In organisations, we may talk about the importance of trust but we rarely focus on what it really means to us, and why we might try to understand and to develop it. Yet it is one of the core elements of any relationship, whether with friends, colleagues, customers, suppliers, business partners or investors.

I once worked in an organisation where people trusted one another. Where people told the truth, shared information, did not feel afraid of getting it wrong or being a failure. When people made mistakes, they were able to admit to them openly and ask for help. Managers were more interested in what lessons had been learned from mistakes than apportioning blame. Gossip and nastiness were uncommon. People could disagree or challenge each other, knowing that it was done with positive intent. People

> Creating trust is an art. Sometimes we work at it, mostly we do not pay much attention to it – unless things go wrong, in which case problems and pain invariably result.

were open, the atmosphere was supportive, problems were solved easily, there was no need to read between the lines because you could rely on the fact that people communicated honestly and no one was 'punished' for speaking out. Because of this strong element of trust, people worked better and relationships – whether with customers, colleagues or suppliers – were stronger and more successful. It sounds like a great place to work doesn't it?

> It can take a great deal of time and effort to create trust, but only a short time and one action to lose it.

The truth is, I have not worked in a place quite like this (in common with over 90 per cent of people that we surveyed). The story is not true. The question is, could it be? It may seem unrealistic or naïve to expect or even imagine that an organisation like the one described above could exist, but isn't it about time we asked *why* this is the case, and whether it's a situation that we want to continue?

So important, so neglected

So, why, if trust is such an all-pervasive issue, do we rarely acknowledge it, especially in organisational life? Why is it something that we tend to have a *laissez-faire* attitude towards? There are several reasons:

- *It takes investment.* Trust goes to the heart of our relationships with others. We know whom we do and do not trust. If we became consciously aware of it, we would realise that when we first meet people this is one of the things we are checking out about them. We would realise how much we do to create and maintain trust with people we care about. It can take a great deal of time and many actions to create trust, but a short time and only one action to lose it. To achieve it, we have constantly to invest our time in doing those things that maintain and build trust. If we lose it, we invariably have to increase our investment massively to claw it back little by little.
- *It is fragile.* Trust is easier to destroy than to create. This could partly be explained by the fact that events and actions that destroy trust are more noticeable and obvious than those needed to establish trust. Also, people tend to put more emphasis on the trust-destroying events and to be more interested in them, so they become more powerful and influential than trust-*building* events. The media plays a large part in this. Negative, trust-destroying stories are much more widely reported than positive stories. How many stories do we read in the newspaper of people doing successful peace work, compared with the number about people committing acts of terrorism and destroying peace?

2

- *The slate is never wiped clean.* We tend to let our current experiences be tainted by what has happened in the past. If, over time, we have had a series of bosses who we trust, we are predisposed to assume that we can trust the next one. If the opposite is true, we are tempted to transfer our previous negative experience onto a new boss who might in fact be extremely trustworthy. The same goes for relationships of course.
- *It is not simple.* Advances in science and technology far outstrip the advances in the field of human relations. Left-brained logic dominates. Trust is a complex human issue that can be difficult to understand and develop. In the absence of simple, easy answers, we stick to issues that we can understand.

It is a difficult subject fraught with complexity and paradox. Once we mention trust, we raise questions in our own minds and others'. We start to wonder about who we can and cannot trust, and why. We feel that it is a difficult or impossible thing to change, so we do not try. When we think of people with whom we have personal relationships or those we work with, it is difficult to face the idea that we may not entirely trust them, or they us. Easier to ignore the issue altogether.

However, trusting relationships are valuable, satisfying and productive. Whether in our personal life or in business, trust is something most people value. It is at the core of all our important relationships. It creates meaning and connection. It gives relationships the potential to be satisfying, safe and creative. Investing in a relationship where trust does not exist is an empty and meaningless pursuit. Yet trust has a fragile quality that means we shy away from discussing or naming it. As if naming it could suddenly mean we lose it – especially if we talk about it to the person we trust. That person may not feel the same as we do.

In the middle of an intense and difficult project, I was once in a bar with a colleague after yet another long day. We were both tired but high from a sense of accomplishment and camaraderie. A few drinks helped us both to move our relationship along to talking about deeper and more meaningful things. We both opened up. We talked about how much we valued and trusted one another. It was a wonderful conversation. I felt much closer to my colleague having had it, and indeed started to think of her as a friend. This is some years ago and I have often pondered on that conversation. True, it raised the level of intimacy and closeness. It also raised the level of expectation on both sides. The weight of responsibility grew. I felt a bond, a sense of loyalty and responsibility that I could have inwardly denied had we not had that conversation. I am glad we did, for I value the quality of the relationship and feel privileged to be probably one of the few people she totally trusts.

Maybe this is one reason why we often shy away from such conversations. The responsibility of living up to someone's trust in us can be as daunting as it is special and valued. Whether it is someone we work with, a customer or someone who we have a close relationship with, when they trust us they make us accountable. We have to commit to that relationship and make sure we live up to their belief in us. How much easier it is to be free of that responsibility. Of course, this is particularly true if we do not trust ourselves.

Trust starts within

We have to trust ourselves before we can trust anyone else. If we do not have faith in our own judgement about others, we could be misplacing our trust. If we cannot trust ourselves, we are not being totally responsible for our actions and ourselves – we cannot be held accountable. If we do not want to be held accountable then, others will not be able to trust us.

Trust also means feeling psychologically safe. If we do not trust ourselves and feel safe in our own hands, how can others feel safe with us? Others need to know we trust ourselves if they are to feel confident enough to put their faith in us. If we do not trust ourselves, we inhibit their readiness to trust us.

People's readiness to trust others grows with their ability to trust themselves. If you believe you are dependable and reliable and you see yourself as trustworthy, others will be more willing to put their trust in you. This sets up a positive feedback loop and creates a self-fulfilling prophecy. Of course, the opposite is also true. Those who do not trust themselves do not trust others either. Their relationships never deepen and their actions are cautious and guarded, and so their potential for taking risks and branching out beyond the 'tried and tested' is limited.

When we trust ourselves and trust other people we set up a pattern of 'giving' and 'getting-in-return' behaviour. We assume that we can trust others and we want to do so; they want to live up to our expectations, and we to theirs. This pattern is exponential. Think of a rally driver and navigator. When they first start driving together all they have to rely on is the knowledge that they can trust themselves and their desire to trust the other. As their relationship develops so does the trust. This notion of reciprocity is central to trusting relationships. We give something and we see what we get in return. If we do not get what we expect, then we usually doubt whether we can trust the other. People usually do to others what they perceive is being done to them. If they feel that the situation is one of mistrust, they eventually embark on a path of increasing destructive reciprocities that serves to make the creation of trust more and more difficult.

What we talk about when we talk about trust

When we speak of trust we tend to be imprecise in our language and what we mean. We mix trust up with predictability, dependability and reliability. This book is about the most sophisticated and 'thinking' level of trust. We are talking about an advanced form of trust that relies on commitment and action. The table below shows the difference between what we have labelled 'faith', 'predictability', 'dependability', 'elementary trust' and 'advanced trust'. The examples in the table below illustrate the difference.

Faith	Predictability	Dependability	Elementary trust	Advanced trust
• A religious belief: trust in a deity.	• My dog will not bite me. • The volcano will not erupt. • The tree will not fall on my house.	• My car will start. • The shoes I have bought won't fall apart. • The train will show up on time.	• I am safe walking down my street. • My company will pay me every month. • The doctor is qualified.	• My partner will remain faithful to me. • My friends will support me when I need them. • My parents will be there for me no matter what happens.

What we call *advanced trust* is the type of trust that we are concerned with in this book. It is not blind trust; it requires commitment, action and boundary setting. In short, it does not just happen: we have to create it, pay attention to it and actively develop it.

WHY DOES TRUST MATTER?

One way to think about why trust is important is to think about what happens when it does not exist.

Imagine an intimate relationship where you do not trust the other person. You feel constantly on guard, wary that the person is going to let you down in some way. It is difficult to relax; you feel vulnerable, careful about what you do and don't do.

Consider the opposite. What about being in a personal relationship where you trust someone who does not trust you? It can be frustrating; you constantly feel you have to prove yourself to that person. You start to feel let down and disillusioned; no matter what you do you cannot create the trusting relationship you want. Eventually that turns to bitterness, anger, rejection and either withdrawal or the ending of the relationship.

Now consider those scenarios in the context of an organisation.

> **People have an enormous need to trust and be trusted. Many leaders fail to understand that – their organisations will never reach their full potential.**

What happens when we do not trust others in our place of work? The experience can be stressful because we have to watch what we say and do. We expend considerable energy managing how we are perceived, making sure we make alliances with the 'right' people and are seen to distance ourselves from the 'wrong' ones. This situation is not about captaincy and doing the right thing. At its extreme, it is about self-preservation and not doing the wrong thing. The effects for the organisation can range from missed opportunities and unfulfilled potential to complete dishonesty and, in the case of corporations, damaged customer relationships, lost business, failed partnerships, corporate scandals and collapse.

Trust: a human condition

Trust is an issue of which we are all aware. Knowing whether to trust a particular person or situation has always been important to human beings on a primitive level, as it underpins basic survival. At its extreme, misplaced trust can literally mean death.

Trust is something that we become aware of at a very early age. As children, we quickly realise which adults will keep their word, which ones we feel safe being around and which we should be wary of. We know who will make fun of us, who will put us down, who is not really interested in us and which people have our best interests at heart. We know who is genuine and who is fake. We have a raw and intuitive knowledge of this, which as adults we often lose or decide to ignore. Many other aspects of human relationships come into play. As children, we act on the basis of our cumulative experience of the people in our lives. We start to learn the value and importance of trust without consciously realising it is trust that we are dealing with.

Later, our judgement gets clouded by ambition, status, wanting to be accepted by others and to avoid any kind of pain, protecting our egos from rejection or failure. We therefore start to compromise, adapt and manoeuvre our way around people and situations.

We are all familiar with the kinds of situations described. It is something that many of us consciously or unconsciously struggle with in our social and work relationships.

Trust is important because in itself it is one of the ingredients of a meaningful relationship. It also matters because of what it can allow to be created, whether that is a psychologically healthy family life or a thriving business. Humans are fundamentally social creatures and trust is a prerequisite for social cohesion.

The paradox of trust

The paradox of trust is that if we consciously seek it, we may inhibit our ability to create it. Trust is a fragile and precious thing that is gained through actions, not words. The person who talks about how important it is, how trustworthy they are and so on, is the one who is less likely to be trusted. Trust seems to be least in evidence when it is talked about the most.

In our survey of attitudes to trust, we found that those people who most frequently and explicitly talk about trust – chiefly politicians and, to a lesser extent, business executives – are the ones who have it the least. To trust someone we need to see actions to support the words. In developed economies we live in a world of sophisticated marketing messages and spin. In response to this, we have become more discerning in our judgements. We know a marketing message when we see it, and even if is genuine and truthful we are often doubtful and sceptical.

Trust in society and the growth of 'spin'

The role of trust as a foundation for a healthy civic society, as well as an economically prosperous one, has received much attention from academics and writers in recent years. Robert Putnam, an American sociologist, studied the effectiveness of Italian government institutions and the public's satisfaction with them.[1] He concluded that the level of social capital – the shared norms of trust, collaboration, mutual goals and expectations – was a crucial determinant both of the effectiveness of government institutions and of citizens' satisfaction with them. More recently, Francis Fukuyama has argued that levels of trust in different societies have a measurable effect on economic performance.[2]

Much anecdotal evidence suggests that we are becoming far more sceptical of governments, politicians, companies and institutions. According to a senior Downing Street adviser, the willingness of British people to trust each other has halved over the past 40 years. Other studies suggest that this is not a phenomenon unique to Britain but that America, Australia and Ireland have all seen a similar decline in trust. Among the reasons cited are the decline of the job-for-life, greater social mobility, the rising divorce rate, an increase in immigration and a more aggressive commercial ethic. The research does not mention the rise of spin as a possible cause of the decline in trust, probably because it was government funded and the sponsors would be unlikely to suggest that they themselves could be partially to blame for the decline in trust!

Spin is nothing new. People have always 'spun' the truth to make themselves or others appear to be right or doing the right thing. It is an extension of marketing: presenting products or services in the most favourable light and in a way that highlights benefits for the consumer. However, marketing does not have the negative connotations that spin does. When we talk about spin, we are not usually talking about something positive. It has a manipulative flavour. We try to figure out what the *real* situation is.

It is not surprising to us any more when governments and politicians are found to be covering up, economical with their information and spinning the truth. Contemporary politics is full of it: remember the Chinese government's initial attitude to the SARS virus, Bill Clinton and the Lewinsky affair, food scares in Europe (the UK in particular), Tony Blair and Iraq's weapons of mass destruction. We have come to expect this as the way governments are run.

David Blunkett, UK Home Secretary, said in an article in *The Times* in July 2003: 'If there is one lasting challenge for politicians and journalists when the events of recent months have played out, it will be to persuade the public that either of us is worth trusting.' He was referring to the dispute between the BBC and the government about the events leading up to the death of UK scientist Dr David Kelly.

PR is big business now. Its role in government is increasing.

The marketers' response: authentic or spinning the spin?

Ironically, some marketers see dwindling trust as an opportunity to gain advantage over competitors and are engaging in what some have termed 'trust-based marketing'. They say this is more than just advertising campaigns with the message 'trust us', but includes creating positive relationships with customers by being more transparent, improving customer service, delivering on promises and honesty.

So how do we know who to trust, when we live in a world in which marketing, spin and PR are so pervasive? We have certainly had to become more discerning as the messages become more sophisticated, but are we more or less trusting and trustworthy than we used to be? Has our response to more sophisticated marketing, PR and spin been to become smarter, more wily and more susceptible to becoming spin doctors ourselves?

Corporate social responsibility (CSR) has become a determinant of trust in companies. It is now a priority for companies whose reputations and brands could be damaged if they do not take it seriously. Companies like Nike and Nestlé have been criticised for their employment and marketing practices in the developing economies of the world, and are indeed taking action to show that they are socially responsible companies. Unilever now applies corporate branding on all its products as a way of making it clear who owns the brand, and so showing their accountability.

Many companies are jumping on the CSR bandwagon because they have to. There is no real commitment to it. The commitment comes when they do it because it is the right thing to do: when it fits with their values and is an authentic step. Otherwise, it is just another policy set in place to keep them out of trouble and to maintain a good image.

Real wisdom comes in the realisation that we need to go back to core values. We need to take another look at what is really important. Many books on leadership have talked about the importance of just being human. This is simple yet profound. Maintaining trust in our complex world is about staying in touch with the simple truths about people. We want to find meaning in our relationships, we want understanding and empathy, and we want to feel psychologically secure. Organisations would do well to take note of this as this applies not only to the people that work in them but their customers and stakeholders.

THE FUNDAMENTALS OF TRUST

We tend to trust people if they do what they say they are going to do, if they practise what they preach and if they tell the truth. These are the building blocks of trust, but they are not enough to create durable, positive, trust-based relationships, particularly in organisations. As well as having leaders with personal integrity there are other important elements.

The building blocks of trust

Authentic communication

People need to feel that they are being told the truth, even if they do not like what they hear; it is crucial to have transparency at all levels and up and down the organisation. Telling the truth, admitting mistakes and giving honest feedback are all also important.

Competence

The organisation needs people who are skilled and competent at what they do. This gives people faith in and respect for each other's abilities.

Supporting processes

If the processes in an organisation are based on the assumption that people cannot be trusted (for example, checking time-sheets and monitoring emails), trust will be undermined.

Boundaries

Controlling people destroys trust, but clearly within organisations there has to be agreement about what people will achieve and how they will do it. A framework of agreed goals allows people *freedom within that boundary.*

Contact

Personal contact is important because people need to get to know and understand each other to build and maintain trust.

Positive intent

Human beings intuitively sense the inauthentic. We know when someone's intention is questionable. For trust to exist it is important that we believe that the intent is positive, even if a person does something that undermines trust in some way. Paul Walsh, CEO of Diageo, quoted in *Harvard Management Update*, talks about the 'assumption of positive intent' or API.[3] He comments that: 'I try to show people that if anybody disagrees or has a violently opposed argument or fundamentally thinks another person is wrong, that the basis for their assumption is positive intent for the good of the organization.'

Forgiveness

If people are to trust each other then the organisation has to forgive genuine mistakes, otherwise over time the effect will be that people will not risk doing anything new or different – and the organisation will suffer as a result.

Trust is not something that just happens or doesn't. It requires a conscious commitment and ongoing attention. It is dynamic: it can be lost and it can be increased. Things regularly happen to compromise trust so it cannot be taken for granted.

It is not a mystical property that we have no control over. If we want it, we have to decide to give it and to commit to it.

The different contexts of trust

What is trust? How do we define it? It is something that we find hard to put into words, something we can more easily define by its absence than its presence. It is so obvious to us when we have it and yet so hard to define or describe.

Trust is not an absolute. It is contextual and dynamic. The constituents of trust are the person giving it, the recipient (this can be a person, a group of people or an institution) and the specific context in which trust is conferred.

The different types of trust at play in different situations are:

- *Self-trust.* This is the trust that people need to be confident of their capabilities and judgements in given situations. Self-trust is central to the ability to create trust because if people do not trust themselves it is unlikely that others will trust them. Mistrust is often a projection of missing self-trust.
- *Relational trust.* This is the trust a person puts in another person or group of people. This is a generalised type of trust and is usually established over time. It is not about trusting people to do something in

particular; it is believing that they have integrity and honesty. If someone you trusted sold you a car that broke down the following week, you would assume your friend did not know that there was anything wrong with it; your basis of trust has been established by evidence that you can rely on this person. Whereas if someone you had only met once sold you a car, if it then broke down you would probably assume that person was untrustworthy and had knowingly sold you a faulty car.

- *Structural trust*. This is the trust that we put in entire institutions, companies and brands. For example we may trust a country like Switzerland because of its history of being neutral, of creating one country from several different nationalities and doing it in a way that has created a safe place. You trust that *overall* the systems, policies, forms of governance and processes have integrity and can be trusted.
- *Transactional trust*. This is trust that is specific, often one-off and pertains to a particular context at a particular time. For example, you trust the travel agent's assurance that when you show up at the airport there will be a seat booked for you on the particular flight that you chose. This is a one-off situation where you only need to trust in the short-term to fulfil a particular need.

Is trust culture specific?

According to research by David Halpern of the Downing Street Strategy Unit, people of different nations vary significantly in the degree to which they trust others. In the research, they asked the question 'Generally speaking can others be trusted?' Scandinavians (Norway, Sweden and Denmark) were the most trusting, with nearly 70 per cent of people saying that they could trust others. Respondents in the USA, Britain and France were the least trusting, with less than 30 per cent saying that they trusted others. There could be a variety of reasons including:

- degree of ethnic diversity/homogeneity
- levels of crime
- levels of geographic and social mobility
- unemployment and job security rates
- poverty levels
- significant trust-destroying events such as health scares or political scandals
- influence of TV and media
- influence of popular culture.

The difference could also be explained by examining the varying values, norms and orientations of the cultures concerned.

Fons Trompenaars' work on cultural diversity sheds light on this subject.[4] He explains such differences by examining how cultures relate to each other.

Universalism versus particularlism

For universalists, rules and procedures are applied consistently, whereas the relationship and flexibility are more important for particularists. In a particularist business environment such as Japan, there is more emphasis on the relationship than the contract. To stress the importance of the contract might seem to imply that the other party will cheat unless legally prevented from doing so. For the particularist culture the building the relationship and developing trust is more important than any codification of agreement.

Individualism versus communitarianism

In individualist cultures, people are more self-oriented than community-oriented. The individualistic culture emphasises individual freedom and responsibility. The communitarian culture puts more weight on working for the interests of the group.

Neutral versus emotional

The convention in neutral cultures is to see work relationships as detached. This is the case in North American and Western European cultures. In other cultures emotions are seen as having a place in business and are displayed all over the place.

Specific versus diffuse

This is about how much we get involved in the specific versus multiple areas of each other's lives. In specific cultures people segregate the task relationship. It is essentially about the extent to which we put barriers around the different areas of our lives.

In many cultures, a diffuse relationship is necessary before people can do business. When they get to the point of making deals, they trust their counterparts because they have allowed them into diffuse areas of their lives and developed relationships with them. This can become more important than the superiority of the product or service that they are trading.

Trust is a complex and multi-layered issue. What it means to you, and whether and whom you trust, depends on the context you are in, your previous experience and your interpretation of that experience as well as your values and beliefs. In the next chapter we explore the principles of trust in greater detail, highlighting what, when and how we need to act to actively develop trust.

A Fresh Perspective

Robin Hobbes, Psychotherapist

Trust is very important to psychotherapists. Psychotherapy does not really work unless the patient trusts the therapist, so we pay a lot of attention to establishing a relationship that encourages trust. Yet psychotherapy has at its heart a profound truth: what is at the core of trust is the ability to trust oneself. We have to move from perceiving trust as something outside us to realising it is something within us. At the outset, patients put their trust in therapists and may ascribe all sorts of capacities and qualities to them. They trust that the therapist will make them 'better'. In reality, it is the patients who do this.

I remember one young woman who was finding the normal stresses and strains of life extremely challenging and hesitantly approached me for therapy. She was both deeply suspicious and highly idealising of me. One minute she would say: 'You must have everything sorted. You know what to do – tell me.' A few minutes later she might attack me for not telling her 'the answers'. She would then see me as an exploitative person who was only interested in getting paid by her. She wondered whether she had chosen an inadequate therapist and considered finding someone who 'really knew how to help people'. Then something shifted in her, at her centre. She started to trust herself, to believe in herself. Maybe I helped by seeing her as being able to trust herself from the beginning, and held back from saying things that might imply that I thought she could not do so. Maybe it was because I was predictable, stable and not attacking her as she attacked me, demonstrating that I was trustworthy. An inner sense of security seemed to flower within her. She no longer saw her sense of trust as dependent on others. Her trusting of the world began primarily to rest in her trusting herself, her perceptions and her feelings. 'I know what's what,' she would say. This is what I mean by moving from seeing trust as something 'out there' to finding that it is within. When we realise this, there results a profound sense of inner security.

We will also explain why trust matters, what can be achieved when it genuinely takes hold and how it benefits individuals and organisations.

2   The power of trust

For trust to take hold, benefiting individuals and organisations, its value needs to be fully recognised and understood. This chapter explores the power and value of trust: why it is important, where and when it matters.

TRUST AND ORGANISATIONS

When considering trust as an organisational and individual issue, there is one fundamental question to consider: why bother with trust? After all, many business fortunes have been made, organisations thrive and people succeed without unduly emphasising trust. It is seen as a hygiene factor: vital and universal.[1] Why not simply avoid or ignore trust as an issue altogether?

Quite apart from the many ethical complexities of this question, there are two practical and interrelated answers to the broad issue of why trust is important.

> Trust underpins our success in many ways. Indeed, it is precisely because it is so ubiquitous that we take it for granted. Breaking this habit requires understanding of why, where and when trust has the greatest impact.

- *Because it is a potential source of advantage* for individuals and organisations. In a constantly competitive environment, this matters in many, many ways for both people and the organisations they work in, as we shall see later. Furthermore, not paying attention to trust also means missing out positive benefits: the economist's opportunity cost argument. This is because trust provides opportunities that can otherwise be lost. According to the *Harvard Management Update*: 'Trust may be just as important a determinant of economic prosperity as physical capital, if only because it allows people in organizations to work together more effectively.'[2]

- *Because it is increasingly expected – and without it we suffer*. Trust is a fundamental human need. People expect their relationships with employers, colleagues, customers, suppliers, stakeholders, friends and others to have a significant element of trust. It is true to say that trust *is* largely seen as a hygiene factor, but often not by those people responsible for ensuring its presence! If the significance of trust is not explicitly understood and if attention is not paid to its value (for example, in times of change, uncertainty, pressure or complexity), then trust can be lost, and the business or individual suffers as a result.

The business writer and academic Professor Nirmalya Kumar, writing in *Harvard Business Review*, recognises the commercial benefits of trust:

> By developing trust, manufacturers and retailers can exploit their complementary skills to reduce transaction costs, adapt quickly to marketplace changes, and develop more creative solutions to meet consumers' needs. Success in rapidly changing environments will go to those who learn to make the leap of faith. [3]

THE IMPACT OF TRUST

Trust results in many benefits: it is essential to leading, communicating, building relationships with customers, suppliers and others, and enhancing efficiency. It is analogous to a car engine: not only do you need it to go forward at all but the more powerful it is the better will be your performance. So, exactly when is trust most valuable, both for individuals and organisations?

> An organisation that actively values and builds trust can organise itself more flexibly, resulting in more, high-quality effort from individuals and teams; moreover, the organisation can cascade trust and its benefits to lower levels.

Credibility and better leadership

The first reason trust matters is because it provides credibility and more effective leadership. Simply put, it brings out the best in people, and it does this in several ways.

Trust is inspiring

When you trust people, you can inspire them to be all they can be. When people trust each other, they are much more likely to get immersed in their jobs, passionately working to achieve their goals and prove their ability. If someone says to you 'I think you will do well at this' or 'You can do it', your natural response is to prove them right, to throw yourself into the task and justify their support. Have you ever worked for an organisation where you were trusted to succeed? Trust spreads, flowing between the manager, the team and anyone else involved in the challenge. The result is invariably sustained commitment and a virtuous cycle, with trust leading to greater effort, which in turn results in greater trust and a higher chance of success. Regardless of whether the goal is fully achieved or not, the individual who tries has a greater chance of maintaining that trust and attaining goals. After all, success is more likely to come to those who are committed and supported than those who are not.

Sport provides many examples of the inspiring power of trust. A talented individual is given a run in the team, often because the coach realises that he or she has the innate ability to compete at the highest level, but may simply lack the confidence or experience. If these elements are introduced and the coach's belief is sustained, then the player is likely to succeed more quickly. There are two contrasting ways of being that are important when achieving success: being masterful and being sympathetic. What trust provides is the ability to access the right pattern of behaviour at the right time: confident, action-oriented mastery or more reflective, considered sympathy, either for oneself or others.

Trust increases productivity

Trust frees people by moving politics out of the way and reducing personal risk. The benefits of trust are perhaps better understood if one considers what happens in its *absence*. Rumours circulate, corridor whispers and after-hours gripes develop, people become uncertain, concerned, confused and ultimately demotivated: a fertile ground for failure, recrimination and a cycle of despair. The amount of time and productivity that is lost when people gather to gossip and discuss what might have been said is immense. The good news is that the opposite is also true: the benefits that can be gained when people are freed to work to a direction and in a way that feels right for them are just as great.

Trust increases competitive advantage

Luxury hotels provide an example of the inspiring power of trust. In a highly competitive environment, hotels at the top end of the market know that the key to success is giving their customers whatever they want, whenever they want it. Given that guests may (and frequently do) have a myriad of unusual, individual requests when trying to make themselves comfortable away from home, the solution for the most competitive hotels is not to try to prescribe what can and cannot be provided. Instead, firms have discovered that the best approach is to tell employees that they are working for the best hotel in the world, and ensure they have the authority to meet the needs of each individual customer, trusting that they will act in the best interests of the client and the hotel.

Trust improves communication and mutual understanding

Without trusted leadership, people may be uncertain about where they are heading, whether in fact it is the right direction, how they are getting there and what it means for them. Trust is the antidote: it gives people the confidence to voice and ultimately resolve their concerns; it allows them to focus and collaborate effectively. To find an example of the clarity provided by trust, simply look back over your career and ask: who do you respect most, and why? Who were the best leaders and what was it that made them so good? It is highly probable that they possessed a clarity and ability to communicate that you could rely on. The alternative, an absence of trust, results in suspicion and confusion as underlying motives are discussed and 'second-guessed'.

Trust reduces stress

Trust maintains pressure but reduces stress; this provides the time and space people need to succeed and provides other benefits, such as improved quality. Pressure is not necessarily pleasant but it is beneficial, resulting from such factors as deadlines and objectives, and creating a tension and focus for our efforts. Trust is valuable because those that have it can maintain positive pressure without causing the negative effects of stress. This is because such leaders are trusted to be reasonable, positive, to do the right thing and above all to be supportive. This then generates other benefits as by-products. So, for example, trust improves quality because people who trust each other are more open and likely to collaborate: improved quality is a frequent by-product, thriving in conditions of trust.

> Trust builds trust, as people respond positively to colleagues who are engaged, engaging and enthusiastic. In this way, the benefits of trust escalate, leading to more robust and valuable relationships.

Trust builds trust

It attracts and retains the best people and spreads throughout the organisation. Implicit in trust are the qualities of openness and understanding: to trust someone you need to perceive their values and motives, and these need to be constant. Because of this aspect of trust, new employees are more likely to understand quickly where they fit in, what their priorities are and how these can be achieved, make the right connections and work in tune with other people in the organisation.

Also, people move jobs for many reasons but two predominate: remuneration is one; but more significant are issues of personal, organisational and strategic trust. People leaving organisations for reasons other than remuneration, career change or personal factors often depart for one of three reasons:

- They do not trust the organisation's goals, strategies and approach. The business formulae or 'ends' are seen as flawed.
- They do not trust the way that things are being done, believing the processes and 'means' are weak or undesirable.
- They do not trust the people working in the organisation, in particular their boss, and feel unhappy. Or, they do not believe the people leading the organisation will provide them with the career opportunities they are seeking.

An atmosphere of trust thus ensures that people work together effectively and are less likely to leave. Unsurprisingly, perhaps, the effect of an atmosphere of trust and trusted leadership is to increase efficiency, making the whole greater than the sum of the parts. An absence of trust results in inefficiency in many ways: as talented people depart, for example, taking their knowledge and expertise, while the company incurs further costs in finding replacements and bringing them up to speed.

Trust delivers lower costs and greater efficiency

Trust lowers costs over a longer period by fostering a culture of cost-control and reduction. Trust can reduce costs by ensuring that people more readily understand and accept current realities and priorities. This highlights the need for the leadership of a firm to share information and build trust with their employees and unions, so that both sides work to improve cost-efficiency.

Trust leads to greater risk-taking

Building competitive advantage is not only about doing your best to attract and satisfy customers; it is about attracting and satisfying them more than the competition does. This invariably requires decisions to be bold, innovative and audacious – that is, cleverer than the competition. Trust is critical because if it is to innovate an organisation must encourage people to challenge accepted norms. A corporate culture that encourages and allows this is fundamental.

TRUSTED LEADERSHIP IN PRACTICE

An example of a trusted and highly effective leader is Nissan's CEO Carlos Ghosn. Born in Brazil in 1954, he joined Renault in 1996 and became CEO of Nissan in 1999 when the two carmakers formed an alliance. He has presided over the revival of Nissan in Japan, and is due to become CEO of both Renault and Nissan in 2005 when Louis Schweitzer, CEO of the French group, hands over to him. Carlos Ghosn identifies four vital elements of trusted leadership, particularly during a time of rapid global change:

- the ability to manage cross-culturally
- a commitment to performance
- consistently living by clearly stated values
- transparency.

The ability to manage cross-culturally

This makes it possible to get the best out of people, whatever their nationality or background. It is particularly significant for someone facing the challenge of combining strong French and Japanese national cultures, but cross-cultural management also matters because globalisation involves associating with people (most notably customers) from many different backgrounds. Valuing cultural differences engenders rapport that in turn develops trust. Ghosn identifies the ability to 'exchange best practices, without any one culture being considered as the reference' as a critical factor both for performance and for achieving trust, motivation and commitment.

A commitment to performance

The determination to achieve the best results is another essential element of corporate leadership, informing an organisation's strategy, choices and key decisions. This involves not just short-term performance but all aspects that determine future financial strength. In short, if customers, shareholders, employees, partners and suppliers trust the organisation's commitment to do well, as made explicit in their strategy and actions, then success is more likely.

Consistently living by clearly stated values

Too often leaders espouse corporate values or missions, only to compromise or ditch them when times change. (This is one of the several disappointing tendencies highlighted by the examples of WorldCom and Enron, where discredited leaders would often surreptitiously ditch their espoused principles – if they ever had any.) Ghosn believes that living by stated values is particularly important during times of change, and he cites the example of the Renault–Nissan alliance signed in March 1999. The stated priority at the time was to boost performance through synergies between the two companies, while at the same time he stressed the importance of keeping their separate brand identities, which were key assets. This was initially viewed with deep scepticism, yet he believes that one of the reasons the alliance succeeded so quickly is that people recognised that everything was done according to these consistently and clearly stated values.

When it came to challenging past practices and attitudes – one of the toughest leadership tasks – consistent and clearly stated values were vitally important. Within Nissan, Ghosn was able to challenge many Japanese corporate traditions by putting the aim of improving performance above other values such as lifetime employment or the long-standing seniority system for promotions. As he puts it: 'As long as people know that you're sticking to stated values, they accept it.'

Transparency

This is closely linked with the previous elements of trusted corporate leadership, and to Carlos Ghosn this means: 'You say what you think and you do what you say'. Only a limited, brittle, paper-thin form of transparency can be achieved through regulation. Without a belief that executives are genuinely upholding the spirit as well as the rules of transparency, it will be of very limited value and use. An example of transparency is provided by Nissan's revival plan, developed immediately Ghosn took over the reins.

> In October 1999 I said outright that we're going to reduce headcount by 21,000, close five plants in Japan and reduce the number of suppliers by 50 per cent. But I explained why, I explained how and I explained for what benefit.

The leadership made specific promises for profitability and debt reduction, and promised to resign if these promises were not delivered. 'I don't say it was easy, but we announced outright that there would be some hard times, that we'd try to do everything we could to make it as soft as possible on people but that there were limits,' he recalls. 'The fact that we did this openly from the beginning was the essential condition to make the plan successful and transform the company very quickly.'[4]

> **Transparency means saying what you think and doing what you say. It is the basis for credibility and acceptance – and it is essential for trusted leadership.**

Innovation

Trust, indirectly but significantly, increases innovation. Where it is lacking, people feel they have to examine and justify their actions. Instead of finding and doing the right thing, developing exciting new ideas, taking risks and adding value, they spend their time toiling in an atmosphere of distrust. How will their actions be perceived? How will they be justified? Who will criticise and what might be the consequences – not just for the idea but *personally* for the individual – of this criticism? With such high-pressure distractions, it is little wonder that creativity is stifled.

At the heart of any enterprise is the capacity to take risks, and to do this successfully requires trust and support. Capitalism works on the simple basis of competition. It requires a product to be better than or preferable to its competitors. It involves anticipating the responses of a changing and perhaps fickle market that may not know what it wants until it appears. However, when trust is absent, risk tends to be seen as negative, something to be avoided, assiduously managed, minimised or removed altogether. In such an atmosphere, it is invariably discussed with a wary sense of concern, even alarm. This view of risk as bad is simplistic: it fails to take account of the value of risk.

> Trust enables innovation to flourish – and mistrust stifles innovation and risk-taking.

To many people the word innovation conjures up the image of a process that is spontaneous and unpredictable, even unmanageable. The innovation literature abounds with stories of serendipitous discoveries and independent-minded champions doggedly pursuing an idea until they hit the jackpot. Often – as the stories invariably emphasise – the inventors had to persist in the secrecy of their labs against the knowledge and will of senior colleagues. The archetypes of such innovators are Art Fry and Spence Silver, the 3M chemists who turned a poorly sticking adhesive into a billion-dollar blockbuster: Post-it notes. In most of these stories, innovation proceeds from the labs or marketing outposts, not from the top of the organisation. In this situation, the role of management, in the view of former 3M CEO, Lewis Lehr, is 'to create a spirit of adventure and challenge'.

Too often, we fail to trust people in organisations, so it is the mavericks that work surreptitiously on the next big idea. Imagine if we nurtured that spirit, instead of driving these people underground – how much benefit would result?

The role of managers in proactively developing innovation could be more significant and direct if they trusted and supported people to share their knowledge and expertise and work on ideas. The commercial development of the credit card is an example. In 1958, a research group called the Customer Services Research Department at the Bank of America, with the remit to develop potential new products, created the first credit card. It was later augmented by seven bankers at Citibank, who added the key features of credit cards, including merchant discounts, credit limits, terms and conditions.

This development did not result from a market need: it emerged because people within the banking business trusted each other and were themselves trusted to collaborate and use their tacit knowledge. This encouraged them to share and apply their understanding of customers, information and forecasts about economic and social trends, experience with similar product ideas (such as instalment loans) and knowledge about new technological developments to devise a popular and practical service: the credit card. The card heralded the beginning of innovation within the retail financial services industry, leading in time to such developments as ATM machines and the growth of Internet banking.

An interesting example of the positive benefits of trust for customers and ambitious firms wishing to innovate is the rise and rise of the supermarket. After 1945, families in the USA, UK and elsewhere continued to shop almost exclusively at small, convenient local stores. The leap came in the 1950s when the idea was born of a supermarket containing everything the family needed. There was a huge debate at the time about the practicality of such an approach: traditionalists who believed that products needed to be kept on shelves behind a counter were horrified at the idea that people would simply help themselves and be trusted to pay at the checkout. Of course, people could be trusted to pay (at least as much as they could under the old system) and the success of supermarkets has increased ever since at the expense of smaller stores. For many of the first supermarkets, trust was a central issue: understanding and trusting people meant that several firms, Wal-Mart in the USA and Sainsbury's in the UK, could start building strong businesses.

THE POTENT FORCE OF TRUSTED BRANDS

One area where the impact of trust is particularly significant for organisations is the area of brand management. A brand is a design, name or identity that is given to a product or service in order to differentiate it from its competitors. It represents a set of features and benefits associated with the product or service. This definition matters, because a vital prerequisite implicit in any successful brand is trust. Brands are likely to remain a potent force in the future, not least because, in an increasingly unclear and uncertain world, they help customers understand what they are buying or being offered. So, if one buys a Rolls-Royce for example, one can expect certain brand values such as quality, reliability and prestige.

The value of a brand lies in the understanding or trust that customers receive, and in making it harder for competitors or copycats to get a hold on the market. This has several benefits, the first of which is pricing. A successful brand can command a substantial price premium, exceeding the extra cost in terms of production and marketing, and this is derived from the element of trust that a brand provides. Research in the UK has shown that in a large number of instances consumers would be prepared to pay 30 per cent more for a new product from a trusted brand than for an unnamed one.

Distribution advantages are another benefit, as having an established brand can also ensure that manufacturers get the best distributors in terms of quantity and quality. The distributors are more likely to be receptive to a new product from an established, trusted brand, in much the same way (and for similar reasons) as their consumers. This is particularly useful for new products. Again, this is because of the element of trust and reliability associated with brands.

The concept of a trusted brand identity or image is also valuable in reinforcing the product's appeal. The Rolls-Royce brand has a stately identity and is associated with values of craftmanship, tradition and prestige, while Volvo has a different brand identity and set of associated values, including safety, functionality and family-orientation; these reinforce their appeal to their specific market segments. This links with the next advantage: the ability of brands to build customer loyalty, again because of the trust and even affection that they can generate.

Another advantage of brands is that businesses can launch profitable new products with a flying start, by exploiting the popularity and strength of an established brand. The launches of Cherry Coke and Diet Coke are examples of this approach, where the trusted Coca-Cola brand – probably one of the strongest in history – underpinned the launch of these two new drinks. This reinforced the brand still further by attacking the competition, adding another dimension to the brand (innovation) and developing new markets (such as the diet soda market). The benefits here are twofold. First, brands often make it easier to introduce new products by exploiting 'brand equity'. Second, trusted brands provide opportunities to open up new market segments. For example, food manufacturers often exploit their position to create sub-brands of 'diet' versions (as when an established yoghurt manufacturer successfully launches a low-fat product). Furthermore, a trusted brand can enable the product to overflow from one market into another, allowing the brand to spread in popularity. This is particularly the case in industries that are affected to a greater or lesser degree by fashion. For example, the strength and popularity of coffee houses such as Starbucks grew during the 1990s and spread from the American northwest to the whole of the country, and then to Europe and the rest of the world.

> Strong brands that are capable of attracting customers, employees and investors rely on one core capability for their strength and appeal: trust.

Brands can extend the life of a product, as by their nature they combine trust, respect, profile and marketing resources, and this can often be coordinated to inject new life into a stagnating product – or even a whole industry. The example of Danish toy maker Lego producing toys linked with films is an example of this trend. Finally, brands provide a valuable, market-oriented focus around which firms can organise themselves. The brand manager is often directly responsible for what the product offers as well as how it appears to the customer.

Harley-Davidson provides a fascinating example of a trusted, world-class brand. From its beginnings in Milwaukee in 1909, the company enjoyed a long history as the USA's foremost motorbike manufacturer. By the early 1980s however, their reputation and business were in serious trouble following a sustained onslaught from affordable, high-quality Japanese machines produced by companies such as Honda and Kawasaki. Following a management buy-out, Harley-Davidson tackled their product quality problems using the production techniques of Dr W. Edwards Deming (ironically, an American whose quality methods transformed Japanese manufacturing). The next challenge was to win back – and maintain – market share. This they achieved, becoming the leading US bike manufacturer, with an amazing 90 per cent of their customers staying loyal to the company.

There are several methods that Harley-Davidson use to build trust and bond with their customers, and each one combines knowledge of the needs of individual customers with a cleverly judged appeal to their emotions. The result is that their customers trust them and they value this, using it to develop stronger bonds, greater profits and more trust, in a virtuous circle. For example, the managers of the business meet their customers regularly at rallies, where new models can be sampled with free demonstration rides. Advertising reinforces the image of owning a Harley, aiming as much to persuade existing customers to stay loyal as to attract new ones. The Harley Owner's Group (HOG) activities are central to binding customers to the company, and rather than providing trite or cheap gimmicks Harley devotes considerable resources to ensuring that their customers receive benefits that they value. Membership of HOG is free for the first year for new Harley owners; thereafter a membership fee (approximately $40) is payable – and over two-thirds of customers renew.

Despite the global economic downturn in 2001, Harley-Davidson achieved their sixteenth consecutive year of record revenues and earnings. A glance at their financial performance highlights the strength and improving performance of the business (Table 2.1).

Table 2.1 Harley-Davidson's financial performance

	1997	1998	1999	2000	2001
Revenues (US$m)	1,763	2,064	2,453	2,906	3,363
Net profit (US$m)	174	214	267	348	438
Earnings per share (US$)	0.56	0.69	0.86	1.13	1.43
Share price (US$, end of fiscal year)	13.63	23.69	32.03	39.75	54.31
Return on shareholders' equity (%)	23.4	23.0	24.4	27.1	27.7

Source: Economist Intelligence Unit (www.eiu.com).

It might seem easy to sell a product as exciting and appealing as a motorbike. But then Harley-Davidson also manages to get tens of thousands of their customers to keep on buying their machines, as well as paying to attend rallies where they enjoy themselves, make friends, provide valuable customer feedback – and even tattoo themselves with the name of the company! How many businesses achieve that?

Rich Teerlink, former Chairman and CEO of Harley-Davidson, highlights two factors contributing to the firm's successful renaissance.

> Perhaps the most significant program was – and continues to be – the Harley Owners Group (HOG), created in 1983. Begun as a way to communicate more effectively with the company's end users, HOG quickly grew into the world's largest motorcycle club. And dealers [a vital customer group and sales channel] regained confidence that Harley could and would be a dependable partner.

The second factor highlighted by Teerlink was the company's willingness and ability to unleash the ideas of their people. 'I myself didn't have a plan for the company in my back pocket. I only knew that capturing the ideas of our people – all the people at Harley – was critical to our future success.'[5]

Improved customer–supplier relationships

Pursuing power invariably stores problems for the future, and this is particularly the case with customer–supplier relations. There are many examples where power has taken precedence over trust. This is especially notable in the retail industry, with suppliers using discounts or rationing the quantities of high-demand products as a means of getting more shelf space, ensuring that retailers carry all sizes of a product or participate in promotional schemes. This is a power play approach. During the 1990s retailers consolidated, with the result that suppliers are now in an intensely competitive battle for shelf space. As far as many retailers are concerned, it is payback time.

> Being adversarial with suppliers and partners consumes more resources for less benefit than taking a proactive, commercial approach based on trust.

The alternative to this approach is to build close, associative working relationships. The point here is simple and obvious (although apparently not to the firms who prefer a power play approach in the belief that there will never be any backlash). It is that by working with retailers in a supportive way, the suppliers can achieve more than they could by simply applying their power.

In addition to storing problems for the future, exploiting power also misses present opportunities. To avoid both of these problems, the important questions for the retailer are not 'how much can I get out of the supplier?' but the richer, more satisfying questions that will lead to greater, longer-lasting mutual success. These include, for example, exploring how the supplier and retailer can:

- work together to drive sales
- adapt to marketplace changes
- improve quality and delivery lead times
- collaborate to develop popular new products
- develop the expertise and skills of the sales people
- improve the financial performance of each product by improving the value chain.

The role of trust in improving customer–supplier relations is highlighted by companies such as the US corporation General Electric (GE). In 1996, GE pioneered the use of an extranet (a closed network for use by people external to the organisation) in its Lighting Division to develop effective business-to-business relationships. The division established a global network linking with suppliers worldwide to swiftly enable the business to complete all of its purchasing transactions. A feature of the extranet known as the Trade Processing Network (TPN) enabled GE's many international suppliers to download GE product specifications and communicate with GE via a secure, encrypted software link over the Internet. The benefits of this approach for the Lighting Division were swift and significant: the cycle time in the purchasing process was reduced, enabling efficient production and inventory management. GE suppliers became an integrated, trusted part of a global community. Furthermore, TPN was employed in seven other GE business divisions as well as being licensed to other manufacturers to use with their suppliers.

The value of trust is simple but important: partnerships based on trust enable firms to provide the greatest value to customers at the lowest cost. This approach requires recognition that the whole is greater than the sum of the parts. In the next chapter, we assess the costs incurred when trust is weak or betrayed and we explore how to measure trust.

3   The cost of lost trust

Try to be transparent, clear and truthful. Even when it is difficult, and above all when it is difficult.
> (Jean-Cyril Spinetta, Chairman and CEO, Air France)

Trust is universally welcome, recognised and frequently taken for granted, yet its absence can precipitate total disaster. The effects of lost trust are only rarely understood. In this chapter, we look at the consequences of lost trust for individuals and organisations. We also show that the way that corporations lose trust affects their ability to rebuild it.

THE CENTRAL ROLE OF TRUST

Does trust really matter? In a world that is increasingly regulated, with contracts for employees and customers, codes of practice from trade associations and commercial rules from governments and supra-governmental bodies such as the European Union, should we just keep to the letter of the law and not worry about trust?

The answer is no, for several reasons. First, people respond better to those they trust, than to those they do not. This matters if you are trying to achieve anything: motivate someone, sell to a customer, share ideas, generate new opportunities, prevent or solve a problem – the list is endless. Second, formal rules will never be enough. The spirit of an agreement, a positive desire to work in good faith to achieve desired outcomes, is often as important to success as the letter of the law. Given humanity's immense ingenuity, there will always be ways of circumventing formal rules,

> Trust is a common currency, universally understood and valued.

so they should not be relied on in isolation. After all, even the most basic laws only succeed because they have the cooperation of the people. Third, building trust can provide an effective source of strength and, if done better than one's competitors or more than is expected, a potent source of competitive advantage. Trust is also a decisive factor in increasing profitability.

Simply put, the greater an organisation's focus on trust, the more profitable it is, as we shall explain later.

However, even that is not the most compelling reason to trust. Trust is a common currency, universally understood and valued. Although the context in which trust exists may vary – from a personal connection to an organisation's relationship with millions of customers, or from a factory in Cleveland to a bank in Shanghai – everyone understands what trust is and why it is important. In the difficult days affecting the global airline industry following the worldwide decline in travel that began in 2001, for example, Jean-Cyril Spinetta, head of Air France, recognised the power of a transparent, clear and truthful approach. He understood that, in adversity, people look for trust and, when they find it, they value and treasure it. This much may seem obvious, but what is frequently overlooked is the other side of the coin: an absence of trust does not result in a neutral situation. It invariably means something much, much worse.

When trust is lost, there is a high cost to pay.

THE COST OF LOST TRUST

Understanding the consequences of lost trust matters, because the potential to lose trust is always there. Consider the simile of trust and food: an absence of trust is like an absence of food. The potential for starvation is always present, and unless we actively and routinely do something about our hunger then we will suffer.

If trust in an individual is lost, if the integrity of a person's behaviour is called into question, then the results are clearly not good, but what *exactly* are the results?

Tarnished reputation

Negative labels such as 'selfish', 'manipulative' and 'hypocritical' are much longer lasting and resilient than 'selfless', 'decent' and 'open'. If you disagree, consider this: it takes evidence of only a single lie for someone to be labelled a 'liar', whereas to be thought of as honest requires a great deal more than one truthful statement. As we have seen, trust is a fragile commodity, slow and laborious to develop, but quickly and easily destroyed.

> Trust is a fragile commodity: slow to develop, quick and easy to destroy.

There are many notable examples of talented people who have done good work, only to be undone and forever remembered for one foolish remark. Gerald Ratner, CEO of a once-profitable UK jewellery retailer, made a now infamous statement (intended as a joke) that he was able to sell his products so cheaply because they were 'crap'.

Humour is a great way to show openness and confidence, but misplaced humour can be lethal if you are trying to maintain trust. More seriously, Matthew Barrett, Chairman of Barclays, one of the UK's largest banks, admitted to a parliamentary committee in October 2003 that credit cards from a subsidiary of his own business are expensive. If the results of this statement were less severe for Mr Barrett than for Mr Ratner, it may only be because banks are typically less trusted in the first place. Sadly, it is easier to reinforce an untrustworthy reputation than to turn it around.

Even higher profile examples of a foolish action completely destroying trust and ruining a reputation are provided by two US Presidents: Richard Nixon and Bill Clinton. The presidencies of both men, one Republican, one Democrat, had their successes; a point not lost on the American people, who re-elected both men for a second term. Sadly, however, both Presidents betrayed the trust of their constituents and their reputations never recovered. It seems that even achievements as impressive as peace, security and prosperity can be totally forgotten and overwhelmed by a betrayal of trust. (This highlights an interesting point about politicians that emerged during our survey of people's attitudes to trust. It is that we feel especially disappointed and aggrieved if we explicitly place our trust in someone – as we regularly do with our politicians at election time – only for them to leave us feeling that they have betrayed our trust. In these situations, our feelings of injustice and resentment appear to be stronger than ever. It is little wonder that a creeping cynicism about politicians of all shades has grown, and shows little sign of abating.)

The point is that once trust-destroying remarks are made or actions taken, then uncertainty results. The question then arises in the minds of most people: 'If they think this is acceptable, what else have they done for their benefit that I might think is wrong?' As all of these individuals (Ratner, Barrett, Nixon and Clinton) have confirmed, that is not a question you want people to be asking about you.

Negative attitudes and blind spots

Of all the consequences of lost trust, a propensity to make incorrect, inadequate and flawed decisions is one of the most significant. For example, if people in an organisation do not trust their leader's motives or means, then this will massively diminish the leader's ability to complete many vital tasks. Without trust, a leader is much less able to:

- foster innovation and creativity, and exploit synergies between people, especially disparate and distant teams
- recognise and learn from mistakes
- analyse competing options or help others to find their own solutions
- delegate or empower decision making to others in the organisation with sufficient time or insight

- motivate people so that they are inspired either to prevent or solve problems themselves, or to proactively implement decisions
- focus others on the need to adapt to customers' endlessly shifting expectations
- manage in changing circumstances
- communicate
- make and successfully implement critical decisions.

Flawed thinking and decision making

Lacking the right information or people to trust, and with the distraction of an atmosphere of distrust, it is all too easy to make flawed choices. If we lack reliable, trustworthy information or people around us, we are more likely to fall into the 'anchoring trap', where we give disproportionate weight to the first piece of information we receive. This often happens because the initial impact of the first piece of information is so significant that it outweighs everything else, 'drowning' our ability to effectively evaluate a situation and anchoring our decision around this one issue.

An absence of trustworthy information, insight or guidance can bias us towards maintaining the current situation, even when better alternatives exist. This might be caused by inertia, or the potential loss of face if the current position was to change. Sometimes we come to rely on a situation or approach too much, believing that since a business formula worked once, it will again. We need to be able to test, question and verify our ideas, thought processes and decisions, and this requires a reliable source of advice and honest counsel.

Another thinking flaw that can arise in the absence of a trusted colleague or team is confirmation bias. This is when we seek information to support an existing predilection, and discount opposing information. It can also be shown as a tendency to seek evidence to justify past decisions or to support the continuation of the currently favoured strategy. It can lead managers to fail to evaluate potential weaknesses of existing strategies and to overlook robust alternatives. A classic example of confirmation bias is 'the waiter's dilemma': a thinking flaw that is a self-fulfilling prophecy. Consider a waiter in a busy restaurant. Unable to give excellent service to everyone, he pays most attention to those people that he believes will give a good tip. This appears to work: only those whom he predicts will tip well do so. However, the waiter fails to realise that the good tip may be the result of his actions – and so might the lack of tips from the other diners. The point is that we all make assumptions like this all the time, but we are more likely to perpetrate them, often in ignorance, if we do not have the benefit of an atmosphere of trust.

Over confidence and its opposite, excessive caution, are both pitfalls promoted by a lack of trust. If we do not trust our judgement, colleagues or the information available to us, then the chances are we will revert to a position based on our attitude to risk and our tendency to display either too much or too little confidence.

An absence of trust can also lead us into the framing trap, incorrectly stating a problem or situation with no one challenging us, and consequently undermining the decision-making process. This is usually unintentional, but not always. Managers habitually follow established, successful formulas and form their views through a single frame of reference. A trusted counter to this approach is essential. The causes of the framing trap often lie in a lack of trust, and include poor or insufficient information, a lack of analysis, a feeling that the truth needs to be concealed or a fear of revealing it.

> **Defining problems accurately lays the foundations for solving them and this requires time, information and skills of analysis. Above all, it relies on a supportive, trust-based atmosphere where matters can be openly discussed.**

As if these problems were not bad enough, an absence of trust can lead many people to avoid making a decision at all, preferring instead to wait and see. This may increase risk because it prolongs an outdated and inappropriate strategy. Also, putting off real decisions reinforces damaging attitudes and allows time for demotivation and cynicism to take hold. A trust-based atmosphere is more grounded in reality: people feel able to give their views, and recipients feel better able to accept them. This is certainly preferable to some of the flawed alternatives, which can include:

- Escalation of commitment. Often, when a decision or strategy starts to fail, those responsible commit further resources in an attempt to prove that their previous decisions were right.
- Bolstering. An uncritical emphasis on one option. This tends to be a way of coping with difficult choices that results in a sense of invulnerability to external events, especially when it is accompanied by an escalation of commitment.
- Shifting responsibility and other signs of weak leadership.

Reduced profitability

When we surveyed attitudes to the issue of trust, we found that people overwhelmingly believe trust is important for building partnerships and joint ventures, leading and motivating people, negotiating, developing new ideas, sharing information, leading change, managing risk, appointing personnel and selling.[1] However, we also asked (in our questionnaire) if respondents felt that trust was important for increasing profitability, and here the majority response was 'no'. Our survey respondents represent a broad cross-section of opinion from Europe, North America and Asia, and this response highlights one crucial point: people just do not see how important trust is for organisations. The truth is that trust really *does* matter if you are looking to enhance profitability, and it matters in two ways. Trust affects profitability indirectly, because it fundamentally underpins all those profit-boosting business activities that we mentioned earlier (building partnerships, customer loyalty, leading, negotiating and so forth). However, it also affects profitability directly, in a variety of ways – as Gerald Ratner and Matthew Barrett discovered. In fact, to be fair to our survey respondents, when we spoke to people in person about the link between trust and profitability (as opposed to asking them to complete a questionnaire), a majority quickly came to see the links between the two issues, correcting their previous view.

> **Trust and integrity enable managers to face the realities of business openly, constructively and collectively. A loss of trust in an organisation results in a closed, destructive and diffuse approach.**

So, how does trust directly affect profitability? The short answer is: in many, many ways. Four areas in particular highlight the direct effect of trust on profitability – areas where trust must be maintained and areas where to lose trust is to court disaster:

- information management
- motivation and empowerment
- profitability
- sales.

TRUST AND INFORMATION

The way that senior managers and employees use information is causally linked to business performance.[2] Clearly, if information is cynically or selfishly controlled or manipulated for personal gain, then the result is a lack of trust, leading to poor performance. This decline in effectiveness afflicts the organisation internally, with employees simply not trusting their leaders or colleagues, and also externally, with their customers and other stakeholders.

The opposite is also true. If managers display and instil in their teams the right attitudes to using information – for example, proactively sharing information and using it with integrity and transparency – then this will lead to improved performance. Integrity means that people do not manipulate information for personal gain, to score points over others or to justify past decisions. To improve individual, team and company performance, people need to share information, knowledge and insights.

Integrity

Personal and organisational integrity are also prerequisites for a climate focusing on improvement, discussing bad news and promoting transparency about errors and failures. Integrity is an essential component of a blame-free environment, vital for business growth and success. Also, integrity matters if employees are to believe their bosses and stay focused and motivated.

Transparency

Transparency means being candid, honest and open, and it improves performance by enabling people to be open about and to learn from their mistakes, constructively, and to swiftly identify and resolve problems. An absence of transparency leads to people being afraid to mention actual or potential challenges. Consequently, they are discouraged from learning, finding constructive responses to issues, taking preventative action or improving company performance. As Enron and others found out, hiding bad news makes it much worse.

Sharing

Sharing information is also vital for organisational success, and it relies on a climate of trust. For information to be shared, people need to understand what is needed, why it is needed and how they will benefit (the notion of reciprocity), and there must be an atmosphere of mutual support, confidence and trust. Clearly, sharing information is vital: without it, the actions that need to be taken to counter difficulties or generate opportunities will be obscured.

As well as the need for integrity, transparency and sharing, *formality* – the extent to which stakeholders trust formal sources of information – also matters immensely. Formal information gives an impression to customers, employees, suppliers and others that the firm knows what it is doing and where it is going. Formal information is like a report card from school: clear, regular and trusted. When it is absent or incorrect, the result is a massive loss of confidence, motivation and belief – not a situation that sits well with stakeholders.

> **Hiding bad news makes it much, much worse. Information has to be formalised, controlled, transparent, shared and used proactively if it is to drive improved performance.**

Trust, motivation and empowerment

Nowhere is the harm of lost trust more apparent for organisations and their profits than in the area of people's motivation. The difficulty arises because people are essentially inconsistent, behaving differently at different times, even under the same circumstances. Trusting relationships are more likely to lead to higher levels of motivation, and consequently greater success, than relationships where trust is absent. Understanding what motivates people and causes them to behave the way they do is therefore an important part of motivating them to succeed. Consider what happens to a team's motivation when trust in their leader is absent:

- There is no clear example to provide a role model or exemplify the standards needed.
- Motivation is devalued and replaced with arbitrary management control, potentially weakening the organisation's ability to recruit, promote or retain motivated people.
- People are impersonally treated as groups or resources rather than individuals; this in turn results in assumptions being made about them.
- It is difficult to set realistic and challenging targets, because there is little confidence they will be achieved.
- Without trust, motivation declines and in time the organisation's performance falters. This relative failure then sparks a cycle of despondency as failure feeds demotivation and a lack of trust, which feeds more failure, and so on.
- Without trust, remuneration can come to be seen as unfair.

People respond best when they understand what they are doing and why they are doing it. An effective leader has the ability to build trust, sustaining the team or organisation through both good times and bad. Not only does trust inspire but it also provides a clear focus on a desired outcome and ensures that the right actions are being taken (such as sharing information) as well as building confidence, teamwork and consistency.

The price of lost trust for empowerment is as significant as it is disheartening. Empowerment essentially means letting individuals get on with their jobs, encouraging the people closest to the action to make decisions themselves. It requires support and a willingness to remove obstacles and so enable people to put their ideas for improvement into practice. Without an atmosphere of trust, empowerment often fails to deliver:

- a clear direction to ensure that people remain on course
- innovation or initiative, as people are uncertain about what they can and cannot do and where the boundaries of responsibility lie

- a full understanding of what is happening
- a positive, supportive and blame-free environment
- a supportive, collegial environment
- time-sensitive critical decisions, often because information flows are erratic and incomplete
- an accurate assessment of performance.

Trust and profitability

Improving financial profitability relies on building trust. Some of the most useful, practical techniques to improve profitability are detailed below, together with the implication of an absence of trust in an organisation for each action.

Focus on the most profitable products and services (those with the best margin)

If we do not have reliable information that we can trust, we have two problems. First, we may not be able to say with certainty what our most profitable products are. Second, focusing on them might involve redirecting sales and advertising activities, something for which we will need to trust people.

Decide how to treat the least profitable products

Again, consensus and collaboration is needed if a 'rot' is to be stopped. Decisive action is needed to turn around a poor performer – by reducing costs, raising prices, altering discounts or changing the product – or abandoning it altogether to prevent a drain on resources and reputation. None of these are easy in an atmosphere of suspicion, insecurity, blame or distrust.

Ensure that new products enhance overall profitability

New products often focus on market needs or production processes, with insufficient regard to the financial issues of cost, price, sales volume and overall profitability, which are inextricably linked. Again, a collaborative, proactive, open approach based on trust is much more likely to succeed than its opposite.

Trust not only has a role, therefore, in managing profitability; it is also essential when managing cash – for obvious reasons – and when making purchase decisions. Shareholders, managers, customers and colleagues all trust that the best suppliers are being sourced.

Trust and sales revenue

How can firms increase or even maintain their revenues if customers do not trust them? The answer is, they cannot. The cost of lost trust is felt particularly keenly when it comes to sales and associated issues such as brand building, pricing, competing for customers and ensuring their loyalty. When it comes to pricing in particular, the issue of trust is frequently overlooked with potentially disastrous consequences. Several pricing techniques can jeopardise trust and long-term customer loyalty in favour of short-term financial success. *Price differentiation*, for example, is an approach that charges variable prices for the same product in different markets, according to what customers are willing to pay. *Milking* or charging a premium price for high-quality versions of an existing product is another technique that can undermine trust. *Variable pricing* results in prices being reduced in order to stimulate business or being raised to slow demand. This is an extreme measure: the problems lie in explaining to customers why prices are fluctuating when the product is unchanged. Finally, *customary pricing* involves charging the same price but reducing the specification of the product (for example, changing the size of the packet). Customers can find it misleading and resent a reduction in value.

> **Brands enable firms to keep their customers loyal because of the trust and affection that the brand generates. Without trust, customer loyalty and repeat business can be difficult to achieve.**

These approaches are inferior to other methods of pricing because they risk losing customers' understanding and trust. Better alternatives are *target pricing* and *average cost pricing*, where businesses target the level of profits that they wish to generate, estimate sales volumes at a specific price and then confirm that price. *Marginal cost pricing* is also a preferable popular technique that is based on the extra cost of supplying one more item.

Brand management is another sales-related issue where loss of trust can be damaging. The value of a brand lies in the understanding and trust generated with customers. If the trust in a brand is undermined or reduced, it is no longer capable of commanding a substantial price premium. As mentioned earlier, distributors are more likely to be receptive to a new product from a trusted brand than to an unnamed one, and many consumers would be prepared to pay up to 30 per cent more for such products. If trust is absent, this advantage disappears.

Another advantage of a trusted brand is its ability to help customers identify their preferred brands and become repeat purchasers. A classic example is the old adage that 'no one ever got fired for buying IBM'. In this extreme case, even when consumers did not necessarily like the product, they still respected the brand.

All successful brands have trust at their core. Without trust the brand is weakened or destroyed, and the benefits of strong, appealing brands for increasing sales are removed.

HOW TRUST IS LOST

Losing trust in corporations

The way trust is lost matters for many reasons, above all because it affects how we can regain it. The way that firms have lost trust in recent years is remarkable. Granted, private enterprise has never been hailed as a paragon of society's integrity and virtue, but the mendacious approach taken by a startling number of senior executives and firms has surprised even the most sceptical observers.

In the last few years, senior executives at Enron, Worldcom and other businesses in the USA and Europe have been found to have falsified business results, hidden losses and lied about their companies. Possessing information is a privilege in many organisations, and senior managers can misuse it in quite astounding ways. It is first worth considering exactly what it is that these notorious and untrustworthy senior managers actually do.

- *Obfuscate.* When revenues and profits are flat or incapable of impressing the markets and getting the share price to rise (share price performance being an important measure of success for senior executives), then there are at least ten different accounting rules that can be applied to make the numbers look better.
- *'Spin' the truth.* Investor-relations teams work full time to convince investors, analysts and the markets that the massaged figures hold promise for the future.
- *Ensure a steady supply of smoke and mirrors.* CXOs (such as a firm's CEO and CFO) actively lobby the accounting boards to keep the rules flexible – and confusing.
- *Confuse the market.* This can be done by starting a merger or acquisition deal that grabs market attention, and then using the M&A accounting rules to further cloud the firm's financial position. Embarking on complex organisational restructuring and offshore ventures can continue the confusion. It gives an impression of meaningful activity, prudence and planning for the future, without any need for customers or improved productivity.
- *Make influential 'friends' – and squeeze them when you have to.* It always helps to have a friendly, influential (and nominally independent) analyst

who can start rumours to improve your share price or question that of your competitors. Remind your accounting firm – just at the right moment – that the other side of their business, the consulting group, is doing very well with you at the moment and you regard both activities as coming from the same firm. Emphasise to the firm's investment bankers that their loyalty and the support of their analysts is now essential as you are entering a crucial, sensitive period.

- *Use special-purpose corporate entities.* A trick favoured by Enron, which used them to hide debt and documentation, and to create false revenue. They proved notoriously hard to unravel, buying the firm extra time.

- *Produce a proforma report, as well as an audit report.* With the right legalese and accounting jargon, the proforma can be used to emphasise the figures that the CEO wants highlighted, with a story about how they reflect the company's real direction and unique assets. This story and these figures can then be given to journalists, who may just run with the company line rather than doing any hard work or further investigation.

- *Use board members.* Impressive board members with established reputations and credibility add credence to a CEO's stories: so the trend is to get good board executives and keep them on your side.

- *Prepare to bail out.* If things persistently go badly, then the CEO (and possibly others as well) may eventually have to leave. In this situation, experience suggests that three things are often done: an inadequate (ideally non-existent) paper trail is left for others to follow; the CEO gets a good pay out, and shares are managed to ensure the greatest possible financial advantage.

These tricks used to work, but thankfully people are now getting wiser to such tactics. The consequences, however, can be fatal. Enron and Worldcom both suffered grievously from some of these techniques, and the bodies supposed to police corporate governance, notably regulators and accounting firms, have suffered by implication. It may be going too far to say that the corporate governance problems that emerged in the period between 2001 and 2003 hastened economic stagnation, but they certainly did nothing to encourage confidence in stock markets.

The lessons of losing trust

The way that trust is lost has massive implications for the actions we need to take to rebuild it. It is not simply the fact that trust has been lost that matters; the way it was lost decides what the consequences will be and what is the best way forward. So, what are the significant factors affecting the way that trust was lost?

The speed at which trust was lost

This is relevant because sudden or rapid losses of trust can be particularly emotionally damaging. At best, this takes time to subside and, at worst, it can lead to recriminations, harsh words and animosities that deepen the rift in the relationship. An example of this occurred during the 2002 Football World Cup held in Japan and South Korea, when the Irish captain, Roy Keane, had a very acrimonious dispute with his team manager, Mick McCarthy. Keane reportedly felt aggrieved at a perceived lack of professionalism among the Irish management team, and this came to a head when players were asked to train on very hard ground that he felt was dangerous. He stormed off and then reportedly swore at the manager in front of the team. The trust had gone and both sides refused to back down or apologise, and so the Irish captain – arguably their most influential player – returned home without playing a game in the tournament. Without being a party to the relationship and incident it is difficult to pass judgement, except to observe that emotion and poor communication seemed to result in a catastrophic and sudden collapse in trust, and this was then worsened by further emotion on both sides.

With a rapid loss of trust, the best approach involves:

- understanding why the rift occurred in the first place
- doing the right thing to resolve the problem, apologising publicly if necessary
- finding ways to rebuild trust, in addition to resolving the original issue
- accepting that even with these measures, the problem may not improve quickly.

The time between a trust-destroying episode occurring and it being recognised

Delaying action can prolong and deepen the rift in trust. If a trust-destroying episode occurs and it is not swiftly resolved, then the outcome will probably be worse than if it is quickly acknowledged. An example of this is the question that haunted Richard Nixon during the Watergate scandal: What did the President know and when did he know it? Denial and delay can often leave people feeling more aggrieved than the original episode.

The solution is to acknowledge early when trust has been lost, or when a trust-threatening episode has occurred. This may not mean public self-criticism, but it does mean avoiding procrastination, obfuscation or being anything other than a 'straight shooter'.

Whether one individual or a group feels the loss of trust

If one person loses trust then the problem may be confined to that one person, but not always. There are many instances of a loss of trust spreading to other people on the periphery, who then indirectly feel a loss of trust. If a CEO loses the trust of either a shareholder or another board member, this can very swiftly spread to others in the organisation.

The key is to recognise when there is the potential for a loss of trust to cascade over a group of people, even if their involvement has been marginal or even non-existent. Fortunately, the principles of rebuilding trust with an individual are the same as those for a larger group of people.

Whether trust was lost through a single episode or a complex series of events

Many factors can diminish trust, and they are in no rush to show themselves. Consequently, over time, trust can die a death of a thousand cuts. It is important, therefore, to realise that the little things can destroy trust just as surely as the big issues. Also, trust is damaged not only by events but by behaviour as well, and the effect can be cumulative over time. If a loss of trust has occurred because of inaction – not addressing a damaging rumour, for example – then it is essential that this is not easily repeated.

The headlines are often grabbed by the most startling, costly or painful losses of trust, everything from the salacious details of celebrities' infidelities to corporate scandals and disasters. However, the bigger part of the iceberg that remains largely hidden is the gradual, daily erosion of trust occurring every day in billions of relationships. Lost trust does not always – or even often – happen with a bang but with a silent, depressing whimper. In time, this can reach a 'tipping point', a moment when the realisation sets in that trust is gone. Only then does an explosion occur: as a result of the loss of trust, not its cause. It is worth considering that more relationships are destroyed by inattention, complacency or familiarity, leading to a lack of respect and uncertainty, than by a single defining event. If this situation is to be avoided, it is essential to recognise the signs that trust is eroding.

> **Whether the loss of trust was caused by a single action or a series of events determines the intensity of the loss of trust.**

It would be too simple to say that one of the major enemies of trust is lying. Trust is not necessarily destroyed by a lie, where there is no intent to harm or where the intention is to avoid harm. In the next chapter, we explore this idea and consider other ways in which trust is destroyed, examining the enemies of societal, organisational and personal trust.

4   The great destroyers of trust

That lies should be necessary to life is part and parcel of the terrible and questionable character of existence. (Nietzsche)

It would be too simplistic to say that one of the major enemies of trust is lying. Trust is not necessarily destroyed if the intent not to harm accompanies a lie. In this chapter we explore this in more depth and we look at other ways in which trust can be destroyed. We examine the enemies of societal, organisational and personal trust.

> Enron, that peculiar product of overconfidence and nefarious accounting practices, created a world almost entirely in its own image. Enron was eventually run on sheer nerve and boundless ego and a particular self-enclosed, self-serving worldview. As long as they kept believing in their own story and as long as they kept running ahead of their fiscal realities, they could pretend they were kings of the world. This kind of self-inflation leads to an endless kind of running and a strange, calculated, and artificial language to explain away anything that doesn't fit the self-created scenario. It could look at the surrounding forest and see only Enron trees, an Enron universe, and an Enron market it was sure it had created in its own image. That self-appointed image was subject to no check or balance, no countering conversation. It bought and bullied members of Congress; it menaced analysts afraid of losing investment business; it manipulated the media, investors, pensioners, and its own share price; it took California electricity customers for a ride; and to cap it all, it pulled the wool over the eyes of its very own employees. In the midst of all this, Enron headquarters was festooned with banners calling for integrity, honesty, and good corporate citizenship.[1]

This is an extreme example of our time: a corporation so big and powerful that it eventually destroyed itself. An enormous lack of integrity was at its heart. The frightened response to Enron is to tighten procedures and increase governance in all its forms. There is a simpler way. It is to build trust.

Not only will trust protect from such rampant wrongdoing it will build solid and lasting success.

TRUTH: THE ANTIDOTE TO MISTRUST?

Some would say it is naïve to aspire to a personal, social or organisational life that is free from lies. We accept that it is sometimes desirable, necessary even, to fudge the truth, be evasive or even tell an out-and-out lie. We can imagine times where lying saves us from unnecessary pain and hurt. Lies can even help us to avoid conflict or war.

It seems to be a paradox, then, that most agree that lying is morally wrong. We teach our children the importance of telling the truth. Then they grow up and enter the world of work where they learn that telling 'the whole truth' does not always serve them well. Yet one single lie can destroy a person's integrity and can certainly destroy the trust that has been developed in a relationship.

Plato said that lies are not only evil in themselves but infect the souls of those who utter them. His view was that the moral life only had room for truth.

Of course, this is a view seen through a philosopher's lens. The practicalities of life and managing our own psychological and social wellbeing mean that an 'either/or' approach to truth and lying is rarely realistic and probably unhelpful.

Lying is an issue that we dance around. We often avoid the word 'lie', preferring to say 'untruth', 'white lie', 'falsehood' or 'fib'. The use of these other words somehow suggests that the lie is less serious or trivial. They often imply that a deception can be excused because it is justified by its motive.

People lie for many reasons. There are those who lie to protect themselves, like prisoners who tell lies to save themselves from torture or death. Some will lie to protect others, such as the mother who tells her teenage daughter that her disastrous new haircut looks nice. Some lie to bolster their self-esteem, as in those who pretend to be more successful, wealthy or intelligent than they really are. Even the 'professionals' withhold the truth; for example doctors who fudge the seriousness of a patient's condition to avoid distress.

Would we trust these people less if we caught them telling a lie or being economical with the truth? The answer depends upon several things:

- how serious we perceived the lie to be
- what we thought was the intention of the person telling the lie
- our relationship with that person
- the context
- the consequence.

To add further complexity, it could even depend upon where we are from.

Rules versus relationships

In his book *Riding the Waves of Culture*, Fons Trompenaars illustrates the cultural disparities in how we view lies or corruption. He quotes a story by Stouffer and Toby.

> You are riding in a car driven by a close friend. He hits a pedestrian. You know that he was going at least 35 miles per hour in an area of the city where the maximum allowed speed is 20 miles per hour. There are no witnesses. His lawyer says that if you testify under oath that he was only driving 20 miles per hour it may save him from serious consequences.
> What right has your friend to expect you to protect him?[2]

Trompenaars reports the different perspectives of the 'universalists' (those for whom rules take primacy over relationships) and the 'particularists' (those for whom relationships take primacy over rules). See Chapter 1 for more detail on these two orientations.

He reports that time and time again in the workshops he runs, the universalists' response is that as the seriousness of the accident increases so the obligation to help their friend decreases. He interprets their point of view as 'the law was broken and the serious condition of the pedestrian underlines the importance of upholding the law'. This suggests that universalism does not actually exclude particularism but that it forms the first principle in moral reasoning.

He notes that, in contrast, particularist cultures are more likely to support their friend as the pedestrian's injuries increase. Their reasoning appears to be 'my friend needs my help more than ever now that he is in serious trouble with the law'. Universalists would regard such an attitude as corrupt. They would see that if people started telling lies to 'protect' one another like that, then eventually there would be a break down in social order. Particularists, on the other hand, would say that where society is based on a code of friendship and a high regard for relationships, this would mean that people are less likely to commit crimes against one another in the first place.

Whether you hold a particularist or universalist view, then, determines what you perceive as corruption.

> Lying is an issue that we dance around. We often avoid the word 'lie', preferring to say 'untruth', 'white lie', 'falsehood' or 'fib'. The use of these other words somehow suggests that the lie is less serious or trivial. They often imply that the deception can be excused because it is justified by its motive.

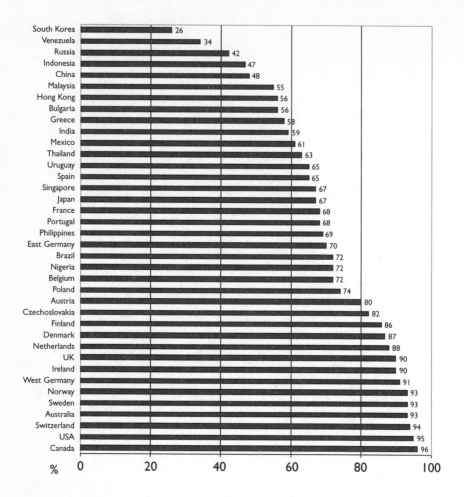

Figure 4.1 The car and the pedestrian: percentage of respondents opting for a universalist system rather than a particular social group

Source: Trompenaars, *Riding the Waves of Culture.*

Trompenaars goes on to give a vivid example of how these two orientations play against one another:

In a workshop we were giving some time ago we presented the dilemma. There was one British woman, Fiona, among the group of French participants. Fiona started the discussion of the dilemma by asking about the condition of the pedestrian. Without that information, she said, it would be impossible to answer the question. When the group asked her why this information was so indispensable, Dominique, an employee of a French airline, interjected: 'Naturally it is because if the pedestrian is very seriously injured or even dead, my friend has the absolute right to my support. Otherwise, I would not be so sure.' Fiona, slightly irritated but still laughing, said: 'That's amazing. For me it is absolutely the other way around.'

This example illustrates how our response is guided by one of the two principles.

We all have our own internal moral code as well as, to a greater or lesser extent, the code that we take on from the culture in which we live.

In Western economies though, there is an increasingly strong individual-istic attitude. People travel more and are exposed to other cultures and ways of doing things. Personal development leading to self-awareness is much more common; indeed you could argue it is becoming commoditised. So people are much more aware of what drives them to behave as they do and the choices they have as individuals. That is not to downplay the influence of our heritage and culture but to say that we can now view them more objec-tively and make choices about which parts we like and dislike. Yet, amazingly, we often fail to perceive or acknowledge the things that we do or that are done to destroy trust. The remainder of this chapter looks at some of the destroyers of trust in society, organisations and between people.

WHAT IS HAPPENING IN SOCIETY THAT IS DESTROYING TRUST?

PR: public enemy number one?

From its beginnings in the early part of the twentieth century, public rela-tions (PR) has grown into a multi-billion dollar industry and has become part and parcel of modern life.

One of the early pioneers of PR was Edward Bernays. His first forays into what today we recognise as PR was at the Committee for Public Information, Woodrow Wilson's pro-war propaganda organisation that persuaded the American public to support US involvement in the First World War. After the war, Bernays worked for companies such as Procter and Gamble and General Electric where he used his knowledge of psychology in his work. He acknowl-edged the manipulative nature of what he did. One of his more infamous 'successes' was his work for the Chesterfield tobacco company in the 1930s, when he succeeded in increasing cigarette sales by persuading feminists to smoke as a symbol of their emancipation.

In the 1940s, PR really started to take off. Public relations companies started to work on a global basis and many of them began working for governments as well as for corporations.

In contemporary Western economies we have become accustomed to big companies pumping out powerful marketing messages and publicity. We are now getting used to governments doing the same thing. In its pursuit of public support, spin doctoring has inadvertently created suspicion and cynicism. We have come to expect the spin. We do not know what we can trust and so have learned to be sceptical.

In response to our scepticism, marketing experts and PR people have to be creative. They have to outwit us so that our 'sceptical antennae' do not even get raised. An insidious promotional method was born to do just that. It has been labelled 'guerrilla advertising' and was devised by a PR company called Big Fat Inc as a way of short-circuiting consumer resistance. Big Fat Inc employs actors to pose as real people who go to bars, restaurants and other public places and chat to people about how good their clients' products are. Word-of-mouth recommendation is an effective way of promoting products. The smart consumer will have to put in place yet another protective filter against such practices as fake recommendations.

This is creating a public who are 'propaganda streetwise'. That is a good thing and a bad thing. It is good in that we are less easily duped. It is bad in that it is eroding our ability to trust. Apart from breeding a new kind of quick-witted and savvy super-consumer whose first reaction is to be sceptical instead of curious, its cumulative effect on society over time can only be imagined.

The compensation culture

When we think of the compensation culture we immediately think of what is happening in the USA. At its extreme it seems that if a company or person puts a foot wrong someone will sue them. This adversarial approach is spreading throughout the Western world. It is an approach that it based on fear. There is no place for trust in this kind of model. In Manhattan, even getting the post delivered is assumed to be a problem waiting to happen. People put signs up by their front doors disclaiming any responsibility, and therefore any potential legal claim, if the unfortunate postie slips and gets a twisted back or ankle.

Of course, if someone behaves like that towards you, self-protection kicks in and you start to behave in kind. So starts a spiral of mistrust and suspicion. This sets up a situation where even if you do trust someone you want to build in a safety net 'just in case'.

The compensation culture has even intruded upon that most intimate and supposedly trusting of relationships, marriage. It may be sensible to draw up pre-nuptial agreements that detail the arrangements if the marriage breaks down but it is unlikely to build an atmosphere of trust – especially towards the person who suggests it!

In some countries pre-nuptial agreements are a legal requirement. What does that say about the core beliefs and values of that society when it comes from an assumption that you cannot trust people to do the right thing?

Lawyers, journalists and other adversaries

Lawyers, journalists and politicians all have unfortunate reputations for peddling uncertainty and mistrust. They are in the business of finding out what is wrong, what is missing, what doesn't stack up. If they are to do their job well and appear competent, they would be unwise to trust people easily. Their craft is more about cold rationality than human relationships. The tools of their trade are scepticism, observation, cynicism, looking for what is missing and catching people out. We have reached a point in society today where we are losing confidence in these professions. We are wary of them and unsure whether we can trust them. They certainly have a tough task ahead if they are to rebuild trust.

The Internet

The Internet has raised issues of trust in several ways. At a family level there is the issue of trusting children not to access inappropriate websites, run up large bills and, worryingly, to get involved with dangerous characters in chat rooms.

On-line banking, shopping, trading and auctioneering may have really challenged the public's trust in the payment systems used by Internet companies. Fraud is a serious problem and Internet companies have had to work hard at gaining the public's trust and assuring them that they can safely put their financial information and credit card details on-line.

At the level of human relationships in the Western world, face-to-face contact is now unnecessary. There are many positive aspects to this. It has revolutionised our ability to contact people in different time zones. We can communicate quickly and get very fast responses. We can keep up communication with many more people because it is quicker and easier than having to phone, fax or use the postal system. It could very well be a facilitator of trusting relationships as long as it does not replace personal contact. It is hard to build rapport solely on email!

Of course, there are downsides too. How many people do you know who engage in email 'warfare'. Relationships can quickly break down; it is easy to say on email what you wouldn't say face to face. It is also extremely easy to misinterpret messages.

The Internet is thus a double-edged sword when it comes to trust. Of course it is not the Internet itself that causes the problems; it is the way we use it and interact with it.

HOW TRUST IS DESTROYED IN ORGANISATIONS

Organisations: they can't handle the truth

In organisations, truth can be a rare commodity. It is seldom that CEOs have their truth-sayers within the organisation. Many do not want them. But can they trust their senior team entirely if they know that their juniors do not say it as it is and tell the truth when it needs to be told?

In many organisations there is an inverse relationship between truth-telling and career advancement. The most that many CEOs can tolerate is a pseudo-challenger, one who will not be too threatening, will back off when necessary and figure out exactly how far it is safe to push things. Just enough so that the CEOs can feel good about themselves, that they are open enough to invite challenge and that everyone can experience the thrill of having a bit of power.

> It is a sad truth that, in many organisations, there is an inverse relationship between truth-telling and career advancement.

In his book *Good to Great*, Jim Collins presents the findings of his research into what 'good-to-great' companies do that make them so successful.[3] The 'great' companies were those that had achieved cumulative stock returns 6.9 times higher than the stock market over fifteen years, a rate that beat General Electric's twofold. One of the differentiating factors he found was that 'great' companies 'confront the brutal facts'.

In summary, this meant creating a climate where people could tell the truth and the facts would be heard. He cited some unexpected findings;

- Charismatic leaders can be a liability as much as an asset because the strength of their personality may put people off telling them the truth.
- As well as vision, leadership means getting people to confront the brutal facts and act on the implications.
- It is wasteful to spend time and energy trying to motivate people. The key is not to de-motivate them. The best companies have great people who are self-motivated, and one of the primary ways to de-motivate them is to ignore reality.

The emphasis on the empirical over the intuitive

In organisations, we look for facts. We base our logic on information and we do not trust people's judgement unless they can back it up with hard facts. We tend to trust the numbers more than we do the intuition of people.

Of course, this has all sorts of implications that are nothing to do with trust. Where trust comes in is in a situation where we have a very strong intuitive sense of something being right and following up on that: a new business idea that cannot be proved with facts but intuitively seems right, where we trust to instinct about hiring someone who does not have exactly the right track record or, conversely, where something seems wrong even though the numbers back it up. Roger Harrison takes up the issue of trust and intuition, writing in his book *The Consultant's Journey*:

Along with many managers and consultants, I have moved over the years from relying solely on my reason to trusting my intuition. ... I grew up in a family full of scientists and engineers dedicated to empiricism and rationality. Feelings were often hidden and denied. I learned early to interpret the promptings of my intuitive knowing as irrational nuisance or emotional disturbance, particularly when they concerned my own needs or others' motives, feelings, and intentions. It surprises me now to remember that, for a long time, to say something was based on intuition was to describe it as a product of sloppy or lazy thinking. If something was worth knowing, it was worth studying and testing empirically![4]

London's *Metro* is now the world's largest free morning newspaper. Mike Anderson, who made the paper a success, had seen the concept work in Scandinavia and thought it would work in London. He succeeded in increasing advertising rates sevenfold and yet revenues increased. He did not research these changes. He just felt it would work and it did. If it had been based on market research, this amazing success would probably never have happened because the data would have been unlikely to show that advertisers would accept such an increase in rates. Mike trusted himself and his strong conviction that it would work.

In Western business, we have long valued science, logic and data as the only credible ways of understanding. However, there is an increasing recognition that science does not have all the answers or the only answers. In the East, there is more respect for the spiritual in business. It is a foolish company in Hong Kong that doesn't get the Feng Shui expert in when they move offices or have a refurbishment. The Eastern cultures embrace both the rational and intuitive in the way people live and work. In the Western world the interest in the unconscious, intuitive, spiritual – however you like to define it – has been far less but is growing.

In her review of Joseph Jaworski's *Synchronicity: The Inner Path of Leadership*, Dee W. Hock, Founder, President and CEO Emeritus of Visa International writes:

> Written from the heart as well as the head, *Synchronicity* is the story of one man's journey toward the place we all must go in the century ahead. Jaworski's life demonstrates that the immense cultural and institutional change, which a liveable future demands, can begin anytime, anywhere, in anyone, even those who have benefited greatly from the old order of things.[5]

For us to start to trust what we cannot necessarily prove is an important step in our growth and development. And, for those who want to develop something new and create the kind of success that Jaworski did, it means trusting your gut sometimes and taking that risk!

Trusting your gut (or intuition) is not yet deemed a legitimate way of making decisions in many organisations. The truth is that we often do it, but then wrap a logical, data-based argument around what our intuition is really telling us to do.

Process having primacy over relationship

Where we substitute good processes for good relationships there is less trust in organisations. We need an assurance that there is a person, or people, that we can rely on. Even in trusted Internet trading companies like Amazon and eBay, which of course have efficient processes, there is also much emphasis on personalised communication and customer service. No matter how excellent the processes are, people prefer to know that they can talk to a real live human being if they need to. On-line banking providers have learned that and now offer 24-hour call-centre support so that no matter what time of day or night their customers have queries they can speak to someone.

> **For us to start to trust what we cannot necessarily prove is an important step in our growth and development.**

The dead moose on the table

Everyone can see the dead moose. No one wants to mention it. But it just stays there. It starts to smell. The longer it stays there, the more it smells. Still no one mentions it.

The dead moose syndrome happens with problems or issues that people do not want to (or dare not) face. It could be that the issue is highly political, it could be something that the boss does not want to tackle or something that someone may have raised before and been bawled out for.

The problem with ignoring the dead moose is that it sends a signal that open and truthful conversations are not allowed here. Thus the person in charge cannot trust that dead moose issues will be confronted, and the people who work for the organisation learn that they mention them at their peril.

Ducking conflict

Constantly avoiding conflict means avoiding certain issues that are obviously getting in the way of effective relationships and therefore productivity. The longer the conflict is avoided the more mistrust takes hold.

The kindergarten syndrome

This is often most apparent in the kinds of communication that organisations put out to their staff. You have probably seen the kind of email or memo where, for example, they do not give the real reason for redundancies (usually cost cutting). They fudge it with cleverly crafted words. This is not treating people like adults, and the irony is that everyone can usually figure out the real message underneath. Trust is more likely to be built and maintained when communication is authentic, even if the message is a tough one to hear.

Favouritism

Bosses sometimes have favourites, either because they deliver spectacular results or it was the boss who hired them or for some other reason. Favouritism can sometimes also result when the favourite reminds the boss of him or herself in some way: a, usually unconscious, form of narcissism.

In their article The Enemies of Trust in *Harvard Business Review*, Robert Galford and Anne Seibold Drapeau write:

> Suppose that the company's star performer is allowed to bend the rules while everyone else is expected to toe the line. As an executive you may think it's worthwhile to let the most talented employee live by different rules in order to keep him. The problem is that your calculation doesn't take into account the cynicism that you engender in the rest of the organisation.[6]

And finally... the 'management'

It is interesting that most organisations still use the same framework of management hierarchy that existed just after the Industrial Revolution. There have been many varieties of management and management theory, falling roughly into either the 'scientific' or the 'human relations' school of management, but fundamentally the idea of management has not changed much.

The word 'management' is derived from the French word *manege*, the training ring in which horses run around on the end of a rope with the trainer wielding a whip to keep them going. The underlying belief that unites all management schools of thought is that, to one degree or another, and for one reason or another, people have to have an element of control asserted over them to get them to perform for the good of the organisation.

Scientific management is based on the idea that people inherently cannot be trusted and that they have to be controlled, told what to do, have their tasks broken down into small component parts and be rewarded by (usually financial) incentives in order to get them to do their job properly.

The human relations school of management is based on the idea that people are fundamentally self-motivated and want to do a good job. The manager's role is to motivate the workers by making sure that their work is interesting, involving them in decision making, communicating with them and empowering them.

Most organisations are run with a combination of the two approaches, and over the last 60 years management fads have swung between these ideologies. Total Quality Management was an attempt to modernise the scientific approach, to realise its benefits, but to do it in a way that people could support. In good times companies will often favour, and experiment with, human relations approaches such as self-managing teams and empowerment. Then, when times are tough and the trading conditions worsen, close monitoring, stricter performance measures and re-engineering come back into force.

In fact, underlying the notion of all types of 'management' are the assumptions that people cannot be trusted to:

- do the right thing
- work hard
- be committed to the job
- be competent to do the job (or to speak up if they cannot)
- create the necessary partnerships with others.

Some modicum of control is apparently deemed to be necessary. However, trust and control are incompatible because freedom is necessary in order for trust to exist. The concept of 'the manager' by its very nature opposes the belief that you can trust people. The manager's job in most organisations is to control and monitor others and their work. The underlying assumption is that without management there will be chaos. In fact, if you take management away you do not automatically get chaos. You may do if you take leadership away.

If you trust people you are assuming that they will be accountable and responsible and so, within agreed boundaries, they will deliver what is needed. This is not the same as 'blind trust', which is a denial of the reality of the situation. The reality in organisations is that responsibility has to be taken, agreements have to be made and commitments kept. Putting in place these 'boundaries' gets the job done.

There is a company in Finland that is a notable exception to most traditional hierarchy-based companies. It is based on the ideology that most people want to succeed. It allows people to take responsibility and deliver against their own definition of success. The company is SOL Services Ltd. It is a contract cleaning and waste management company. At a conference in London in 2003, Liisa Joronen, its Managing Director, said:

You've got to let people think and decide for themselves. Don't obstruct them with bosses, rules and restrictive working conditions. After all, it is most important that the goals are achieved, and this is best left to people's own initiative and creativity.

Ms Jorenen believes that high customer satisfaction and employee satisfaction go hand in hand and are the ultimate conditions for high profits. Her company is living proof that goals, trust, creativity, continuous learning, freedom, responsibility, joy and business success all go together.

In order to deliver the cleaning services to their customers, SOL organisers and cleaning teams draw up their own targets. Supported rather than controlled by supervisors, the cleaners are encouraged to work on their own and deliver whatever is necessary to the customer.

SOL is one of the most profitable cleaning companies in the world, with a return on investment of 42 per cent and annual growth rates of between 12 and 20 per cent. Ms Jorenen says that the only party that is 'boss' in the eyes of her people is the customer.

> In fact, trust and control are incompatible because freedom is necessary in order for trust to exist. The concept of 'the manager', by its very nature, opposes the belief that you can trust people.

The example of SOL clearly illustrates the impact of the leader on the extent to which an organisational culture of trust can be created. Because it is a critical factor, we have devoted an entire chapter to leadership.

HOW TRUST IS DESTROYED BETWEEN PEOPLE

Lack of congruence

Simply put, when people say one thing and do something else we tend not to trust them. There are other ways that people can be incongruous:

- they smile with their mouth and not with their eyes
- their body language does not match their words
- their words don't match their tone of voice
- they do not live out what they believe in.

Incongruence is not always the result of the person deliberately trying to mislead. It could be that someone has a desire to please or to be liked, wants to fit in or is looking for recognition. The result, however, is often to create a dynamic that makes trust difficult to achieve in that relationship.

Hidden agendas

We usually realise that people have a hidden agenda when their behaviour is incongruous in some way. A hidden agenda is where someone appears to be doing or saying something for one reason but is actually acting from another, self-serving motive. Hidden agendas are the things that office politics are made from. Working in an environment where people are suspicious or unsure of others' agendas results in the withholding of information, spreading of inaccurate information and generally self-protective behaviour.

A management consultant recounted the following story to us.

> I once prepared a two-day senior management workshop for a very large international consultancy. I worked with the practice partner who told me what was needed, vetted the output, checked with other partners and confirmed the first event. There were to be nine such events in quick succession in the UK with the potential for more in the USA and worldwide.
>
> During the event I noticed two participants were particularly interested, taking lots of notes and so on. 'Wonderful,' I thought, 'they are really taking this to heart.' I got full participation from all the delegates and tremendously positive feedback from all involved. Only afterwards did I realise that the two 'interested' delegates were in fact preparing to run the workshop themselves. The organisation dropped me and ran the workshops themselves in their other locations. They could have obtained most of the material I had used as it was in the public domain. It was the way I had put it together that interested them. They didn't have the decency to let me know what was happening. Although I had made it clear to my contact that I was happy to 'transfer the technology' through him, they obviously didn't want to take that on trust, and didn't want to pay me for more than the first workshop to do it. I learned a lot. Maybe I was starstruck by the corporate name, maybe the prospect of a big deal, maybe I took them too much at face-value. But at the end of the day I don't think I could have protected myself from this predatory behaviour.

Lack of authenticity

Being authentic is being genuine. It means saying what you really think and feel and being true to your values and beliefs. There is a robustness about authentic people. We may not always like their honesty but we know we can trust them to be honest and not to play games.

Closely linked to the ability to be authentic is the ability to show vulnerability. All humans feel vulnerable sometimes. An authentic person is able to admit that fact. When people are open and truthful and admit they are unsure, do not know the answer or reveal that they are afraid, this is vulnerability. Not only does it help us to 'connect' to them as fellow human beings (seeing ourselves reflected in them), it enables us to trust them.

Essentially, admitting our vulnerability is being honest with ourselves and others. We are not pretending. We are admitting we are not perfect.

Below the tip of the iceberg

All of the behaviours described above are ones you can see people displaying. They are 'above the waterline'. It is the forces at work below the waterline that offer some explanations as to why people behave in those ways.

When people act in ways that compromise the ability to develop trust, it is not always because they are playing games or are deliberately trying to manipulate. It could be for a number of reasons, which they are often unaware of. For example:

- They may be insecure and feel as though they are not good enough.
- They may have a strong need to be liked or approved of.
- They may want to fit in and will do what they perceive necessary to be accepted.
- They may have strong needs to exert power and control over others.

Behind all of these desires is fear. So much of the behaviour we see in organisations is based on fear of all of these unconscious drives and the need to protect the ego. These feelings increase in cultures where trust is not strong. In those cultures self-preservation is important so people are not going to feel that they can be themselves and show their vulnerabilities. Their main drive will be to stay out of trouble and protect themselves.

If these 'demons' are to be reined in and stopped from preventing the development of trust then there must be:

- awareness and knowledge
- an intention to build trust for its own sake not for what it can produce
- a commitment to actions that result in relationships of trust.

A fresh perspective

Anna Phillips, learning and development consultant

The majority of coaching relationships within a corporate setting are managed on a tripartite basis with the coach, client and sponsoring organisation all having a role and a vested interest in the process. If trust is to be established and maintained within this relationship, the setting of boundaries is a fundamental requirement. It is essential to make a clear distinction between what remains confidential and what is accessible to a wider audience. This is true for all coaches, but poses particular dilemmas for the in-house coach who is subject to the same organisational dynamics and politics as the client; in such a case it is not always clear how to establish and maintain these all important boundaries. The in-house coach has continually to exercise judgements of this kind and to manage potential conflicts of interest, as the following two examples illustrate.

A common dilemma, and one I have faced many times, is the career development conversation in which an individual expresses a desire to leave the organisation. As a coach I have to be clear in my own mind, and explicit with my client and the organisation, where responsibility for holding and divulging such information rests. My view is that this remains privileged information. I will encourage clients to take the matter up with their managers and in succession planning sessions, to discuss the possibilities for meeting their career aspirations within the organisation. I will encourage managers to hold conversations with staff so as to get to know their aspirations well and to reinforce the belief that they are valued by the organisation. I do not consider it my place as a coach to highlight the danger of losing any particular individual. I believe that ultimately what is best for the individual is best for the organisation and I always make this clear to both the company and the client before I undertake any development conversations. Others may well take a different view; what is important is that all parties are clear from the outset about what is communicated by the coach.

It is also very common for the in-house coach to know about and have relationships with people who work with those they are coaching. I recall one particular case when I was coaching someone who changed his roles and reporting line part way through our programme. My client was finding it difficult to establish rapport and build a relationship with his new boss. The dilemma for me was that I knew his new manager very well. She had spoken to me at length about both professional and personal matters and so I was in the privileged position of knowing more about her motivations, interests, thinking and decision-making preferences than most. I can recall sitting with a coffee and preparing for the next coaching session, pondering how much I could and should share with my client that would help him to better understand and relate to his new manager. It was in everyone's interests that an effective working relationship was established, but it was equally important that I preserve the integrity and distinction of the relationships I had with each party. I had anticipated and was therefore prepared for the question that inevitably came: 'I knew this individual well, how did I find her to work with?' I chose to share only what I might legitimately have gleaned from general business interactions with her, such as my perception of her contributions and impact on others in meetings. I was also quick to counter this question by saying that this was not as relevant as his interaction with her, and proceeded to explore with him ways he could gain greater insight and build rapport based on his experiences of working with her.

As can be seen, there is a particular set of tensions and dilemmas for the in-house coach that requires careful navigation in order to establish and maintain trust. These issues are further complicated for the human resources (HR) professional who assumes a coaching role.

While informal coaching takes place right across the organisation, it is often the HR department that undertakes responsibility for formal coaching programmes. One of the main reasons for this is the perceived lack of skill and time for line managers to undertake coaching activity, along with the myth that 'people-related' matters belong in the HR domain. There is also a belief that the HR team has the most up-to-date information on job vacancies, organisational structures and development opportunities, and is therefore best placed to support employees with their development.

Yet herein lies a real paradox, for the HR function is also associated in the minds of their internal client base with stewardship of pay, rations and promotion processes, and the HR department may therefore not be seen as a neutral party. As an employee, are you confident that you can have a conversation about work–life balance, ambition (especially lack of) or career plans that involve leaving the company, and that there will be no disclosure or negative consequences in doing so? I have had many employees tell me they are reluctant to disclose their feelings and views to a member of the human resources team because they do not trust how such information will be used.

It is too simplistic to assume that they mistrust the person but not the function. While this may be true in some instances, I have often been told that the reason was the individual did not want to put the HR manager in a difficult position. I have never encountered this particular issue, partly because I was in a purely development role, discreet from mainstream HR activity. Interestingly, employees would often tell me that they did not associate me with HR, as if this in some way explained their readiness to confide in me. This perception poses a real challenge for the HR function, particularly as the trend to bring coaching activity in-house is increasing amongst larger corporations.

There is of course a counter argument, and I have certainly had employees express a preference for working with an in-house coach from the HR team as opposed to an external one. The most frequently cited reason is that they believe a colleague shares a common bond and interest with them, and can be trusted to do the best by them because there will be an ongoing relationship that does not exist with an external coach.

It is essential to address these dilemmas, for trust is integral to an effective coaching relationship for all parties concerned and regardless of whether an internal or external coach is involved. The sponsoring organisation trusts that the provision of coaching for key personnel will enhance individual and collective performance and indirectly benefit the all-important bottom-line results. The individual trusts that there is no hidden agenda on the part of the organisation, and that the coach is competent and respects confidentiality in the provision of support throughout the development process.

The coach trusts that the organisation is honest and transparent about its motives for providing coaching services. Unfortunately, if you speak to any experienced coach you will hear tales of coaching being used inappropriately as a substitute for good management in dealing with a 'problem-child', or as evidence that the organisation has offered someone an opportunity to improve when the intention is actually to get rid of the individual concerned.

In the coaching role we also trust that the individual client will partner with us and be prepared to push the comfort-zone in the process of personal growth. Finally, as coaches, we have to trust ourselves. The wonder of human nature lies in its complexity and infinite variety and so we must trust our own judgement and intuition yet also know the limits of our ability. For there is a thin, grey line between coaching and counselling and it is vital for us to recognise where our expertise ends and another's begins.

The world inhabited by the coach is an immensely rewarding if an equally complex one. There are no easy answers to the dilemmas faced in the coaching relationship or ready-made solutions for engendering trust. What is certain is the importance of establishing clear and explicit boundaries and overt parameters for communicating information at the outset.

5   How leaders build trust

People look for reasons why they cannot trust the leader more than for reasons why they can.

Most leaders would probably say that trust is important. If you could bottle it, they would probably buy it! However, few think about it very much or do anything to consciously achieve it. There are many reasons for this. Most people do not think about it too much. Some take it for granted, and when they do consider it they feel that trust probably exists for the most part, so there is no need to focus on it. When it is present, leaders do not tend to attribute success to trust. In fact, its existence as a vital ingredient for organisational success is often invisible to leaders. Some think that it is very difficult to do anything about, so they do not even try. Others see no other way than to run their organisations using power rather than trust.

In this chapter, we examine what trusted leaders do, highlighting examples of what leaders have achieved by building trust in their organisations.

YOU'VE GOT TO GIVE TO GET

There is a story of a manager at General Motors in the USA who turned round the worst performing plant in the company to one that was an exemplar of productivity and quality. She did it through involving the employees and showing trust in them. They were suspicious of her at first and did not do the things that they had agreed to do in their numerous discussions about how to improve productivity. When this happened she confronted them openly and talked of how they had betrayed the trust that she had shown in them. But she continued to trust them. This happened several times. Eventually they started to realise that she did have expectations and trusted them to keep their commitments. The plant's performance improved to the point where the decision to close it down was reversed by senior management.

She achieved this astonishing result because she continued to trust them after they initially failed to honour their commitments. She confronted their betrayals of her trust directly and openly. They tested her resolve, realised that she was determined to trust them, moved beyond their suspicion and finally started to meet their commitments and live up to her expectation that she could trust them.

This virtuous circle of trust is one that few managers experience because they are not prepared to stick with it when initial trust is betrayed. At the very moment that they could transform the situation they actually give up, assume that the employees can never be trusted and return to their old control-based way of managing.

Why question a control-based way of managing? It delivers the results, achieves targets and budgets and ensures control over what is going on. But power relationships based on controlling do not result in the best performance. How much better could performance be if managers switched their style from control to trust?

The illusion of power

The basis for power-based management that relies on systems of controlling employees is either punishment or reward. Either way there is an external motivator. In power relationships that rely more on punishment than reward, the more oppressive the systems are the more resentful employees become, or, in extreme cases, try to regain a feeling of power by sabotaging or getting even in some way.

Starbucks is a company that is run very differently from most companies. It is not managed using conventional power-based management methods. Howard Schultz the CEO explains how he runs the business:

> If there's one thing I'm proudest of at Starbucks, it's the relationship of trust and confidence we've built with the people that work at the company. That's not just an empty phrase as it is in many companies. This attitude runs counter to conventional business wisdom. A company that is managed for the benefit only of its shareholders treats its employees as a line item, a cost to be contained. Executives who cut jobs aggressively are often rewarded with a temporary run up in their stock price. But in the long run, they are not only undermining morale but sacrificing the innovation, the entrepreneurial spirit and the heartfelt commitment of the very people who could elevate the company to greater heights.

What is your intention?

Most senior executives spend a fair amount of time trying to get people to trust them. Paradoxically we are least likely to trust someone who tries to get us to do so. We will however trust someone who invests in a relationship with us *for the sake of the relationship.* When people try to get others to trust them, they usually want to use that trust so that they can gain something. It could be promotion, support in a negotiation or getting them to put in a good word to someone else. If you spend time building a relationship, that rather than trust is the objective. People who are accused of being manipulative, lacking integrity or having their own agenda, are often expert in gaining trust for such purposes.

The people who engage in building trust are concerned about good relationships and acting in integrity. The objective is the relationship: not gaining trust for itself but the relationship for its own sake. By its very nature, this is something that the people who do it seldom think about. It is just the way they are and how they operate. Because people sense that this is the case they are more likely to trust them than the others. The others may display very similar behaviours and say the right things. It is often difficult to see the difference explicitly, but it is there. It is one of *intent*. People pick this up in a very subtle way. They may not be conscious of what they are experiencing but they evaluate the manipulative person as someone to be wary of.

Few spend much time thinking about trust. If they do think or talk about it, it usually comes out as at best a 'motherhood' type of statement or, at worst, as trite and disingenuous. Why is this and does it matter?

One of the reasons why trust is not an overt part of day-to-day business talk is because it has to do with people's values and beliefs about themselves and others. Many of us never give such matters any thought, except perhaps tangentially or when something happens that challenges our values.

Values are at the core of what is important to people, and form at an early age. We often become conscious of our values when we encounter someone who does not have the same ones or when something happens that infringes them. The value of being trustworthy and trusting others is something that is likely to remain unconscious and in the background, unless something happens to challenge our trust.

Our authentic intent is rooted in our values. There is alignment between what we say is important and what we do to demonstrate that. Our authenticity is important because when we are authentic we are congruent and so people trust us.

WHAT DO TRUSTED LEADERS DO?

Some think that either people trust them or they don't and there is nothing they can do to influence that. While there is no quick or easy way to become a trusted leader, it is possible to build trust by displaying certain values and behaving in certain ways. Trusted leaders hold certain values, behave in certain ways and do certain things. These are the characteristics that trusted leaders display.

They have insight into themselves

To become a trusted leader we need to be aware of what our values are. We may discover that keeping our word, making a difference to the world and loyalty are important to us. Most of us hold values that have to do with our relationships with people. Even those who do not appear to care about others will usually have a positive intention and have values that support that positive intention. For example, managers who pursue power and try to control others may actually be looking for recognition and confirmation that they are, themselves, worthwhile. The value might be to respect others. Of course, such people are often not conscious of the reasons behind their controlling drives.

Self-knowledge is, therefore, fundamentally important if we are to get a sense of why others might trust us (which of our values they can relate to) and what we do that either reinforces trust or gets in the way.

Perhaps surprisingly, even leaders whose values are more self-centred can develop trust in their organisation if they recognise the ways they act. I worked in a company whose CEO was very controlling and liked to have things his own way. He did not listen very much to others. However, after some pressure from his frustrated executive team, he agreed to bring in an organisational consultant to help change the culture away from 'command and control' and towards a much more involving and consultative one. One of the first things that happened was that he was given feedback by the consultant who had spoken to many people about him and his style. He was asked what it was he did that helped and what he did that hindered them. He was told that he did not listen, he needed to trust them more to do their jobs and he should relax the reins. He found this difficult to hear and perceived it as criticism. At first, he was very defensive. After a while he agreed to the consultant facilitating a meeting for him to talk about the feedback with the executives. It was a tough but sensitive meeting where they talked about the feedback, and what it meant, and eventually he accepted it. They agreed that they could point out to him when they felt he was not listening or when he was trying to force his own opinions. They started to work in this way. At times, he would even leave the executive board meetings when it became too difficult for him to resist taking control and launching into one of his famous monologues. The result of this was that they developed a huge amount of respect for this man who had gained the self-knowledge to know when he was having a negative impact. His basic drives and values did not change but his intention and behaviours did and, as a result, he created a culture that most employees felt to be one of the most open and trusting that they had ever worked in. He also commanded a huge amount of respect, whereas previously people had not respected him very much at all.

They create an atmosphere and expectation of trust

The leaders who cultivate an organisation of trust think and do a lot to make it that way. They work at it – like the GM manager we described at the start of this chapter. She worked hard, and in a very conscious way, to develop trust. She took responsibility for creating it. She did not blame the workers or anyone else for the lack of it. Sure she held them responsible, but she herself took the responsibility for creating a climate of trust.

The ability to create trust is not just to do with how leaders behave. They have to set boundaries and make their expectations clear to prevent it becoming a 'free for all'. Julian Richer of the successful UK hi-fi chain Richer Sounds has developed a rewarding and trust-based organisation that has a waiting list of people wanting to work there. One of his key principles is that the sales staff take responsibility for doing what they think is appropriate to make the customer happy. To enable staff to do that confidently there is an in-depth training programme that covers product knowledge, building relationships, how to handle a range of challenging situations and more. New sales people also have a colleague who takes care of them and 'mentors' them in their first few months. Out of respect, they are all called 'colleagues'. So Julian Richer has set up the 'rules of engagement', as well as putting in place training and support systems that provide a framework within which people can be trusted to do what they consider to be right.

They take responsibility

In his book *Good to Great* Jim Collins talks about 'Level 5 leaders'.[1] These are the ones who 'build enduring greatness through a paradoxical blend of personal humility and professional will'. He says:

> Level 5 leaders look out of the window to apportion credit to factors outside themselves when things go well (and if they cannot find a specific person or event to give credit to, they credit good luck). At the same time, they look in the mirror to apportion responsibility, never blaming bad luck when things go poorly.

The 'mirror and the window' is a useful way of thinking about the difference between managers who blame other people or things when things do not work out as they want them to. They either have an external locus of control or simply lack a robust enough ego to cope with taking responsibility when something goes wrong. If our GM manager had looked out of the window, instead of in the mirror, she would have experienced the first betrayal, blamed the workers and mistrusted them from then on. As it was, she realised that she could not control them; all she could do was control her own response to them.

Their intent is clear and honest – without hidden agendas

This is where many politicians and business leaders really fall down. Even when they have no hidden agenda, the lack of straightforward, easy-to-understand communication can make people think there is a hidden agenda.

Often leaders will fudge the truth or misrepresent a situation to save the face of those in power. Most people know when someone in a company has been 'pushed out'. How often do we see emails announcing with regret that the person is leaving and we are sorry to see him or her go, when we know very well that an arrangement has been made with that person and the company is not sorry at all? This kind of dishonesty causes cynicism and mistrust.

Trusted leaders are open. They say what they really think and feel and, unless there is good reason not to, they speak openly. Of course there are times when CEOs are unable to speak about something because of commercial or personal confidentiality. Ricardo Semler, CEO of Semco, says that in those situations he does not say anything at all. The problem with that approach is that people sometimes fill in the blanks with gossip; it may be better to acknowledge the situation but to say that you cannot speak about it for reasons of confidentiality.

They genuinely have the organisation's and employees' best interests at heart

Another characteristic of the 'Level 5 leaders' that Jim Collins identified was doing the right thing for the company not for themselves. Collins describes what they do:

> Channels ambition into the company, not the self; sets up successors for even greater success in the next generation. … Sets the standard of building an enduring company; will settle for nothing less.

These were leaders who wanted to leave a legacy. They wanted to build something that went on far beyond their tenure with the company. For them, it was about what they could contribute, not what they could gain for themselves. This is rare in business. For most executives their own career and ambition come before any greater purpose. How can people really trust those who, ultimately, would rather pursue their personal agenda than a collective one?

They have credibility

They have the overall capability to lead. This is not to say that they have to know everything or have the answers on all technical or specialist matters. But they have to have the capability to ask the right questions, create an atmosphere where people can talk honestly, bring in the right people and have high standards for how people treat each other. And, they must have clear convictions and passion for what they do. It has to be obvious what they really care about.

They are consistent

This does not mean that they do exactly the same thing in the same way in any given situation. It means that they treat people fairly, that they have certain standards of behaviour and performance and uphold them no matter what. It means that their values and principles are so clear that people are able to predict their response. It is like the child who knows that their mother or father will expect them to write a thank-you letter after they have been given a gift. The child knows this is important for the parents and that he or she will be expected to do it.

Where leaders often fall down spectacularly, even if they are great leaders in other ways, is tackling performance issues of senior people. This can be a major blow to their credibility.

The typical scenario is a senior executive who delivers results but is a terrible manager: one who is short-tempered, aggressive, disliked and disrespected by the staff and creates an atmosphere of tension and fear. But because the targets are always met, the manager gets away with it. The CEO thinks that it would be too great a risk to fire such a high achiever. In fact, for many reasons, it is a big mistake not to tackle the issue: the cost of staff turnover, the loss of credibility among everyone else in the company (especially if 'appropriate behaviours' – or, in management jargon, *competencies* – are enforced among the lower echelons) and the risk of a lawsuit. Great managers motivate their people in an environment of trust and openness *and* exceed targets. It is not an either/or. What is more, they are more likely to have the capability and desire to develop others to do the same. CEOs who let even one misbehaving manager keep a job because of success in beating targets have traded their own credibility and the trust of their entire workforce.

> CEOs who let even one misbehaving manager keep a job because of success in beating targets have traded their own credibility and the trust of their entire workforce.

They trust others

They trust people. They do not rely on power, control and an overload of rules. They believe that people want to do the job well. This tends to be a self-fulfilling prophecy.

Ricardo Semler in his book *Maverick* writes about his company Semco.[2] 'We have absolute trust in our employees, in fact we are partners with them.' Semco is a highly unusual workplace where people even set their own pay according to a number of criteria: their value to the company, what they think they can earn elsewhere, how much colleagues with similar responsibilities make, what their friends make and how much they need to live. Semler describes how they introduced this system and his surprise that people invariably set their pay lower than he would have done. Those who opposed this idea argued that it was a sure way of making the company go bankrupt. It hasn't.

Trusted leaders have confidence in their own judgement, they display an attitude of trust, they assume they can trust others and they certainly trust themselves.

Gerard Fairtlough was the founder and CEO of Celltech, a biotechnology company. In 1989, Celltech's largest shareholder was forced to offer its shares for sale. This could have triggered a takeover bid for the whole company. The Board decided that the appropriate course of action was to cooperate with the potential bidders for the company. It was necessary to maintain commercial confidentiality during this process. Some board members thought it should be kept secret from employees, for fear of someone leaking it to the press. Gerard managed to persuade them that this was unlikely, as the entire operation of the company, since its inception, had been based on the fact that 'open communication depends on trust and trust depends on open communication'. He was willing to stake his reputation on this. They told all 400 employees and asked them to keep it confidential. They did – for about three weeks, until the public announcement was made.

They let others see their passion – and it is obvious what they care about

This is such an obvious one. We are so much more inspired to follow someone if it is evident that they truly care about the project/company/product. But how many passionate leaders can you name? It is particularly difficult to think of passionate leaders in business. Somehow, we have come to believe that passion and excitement do not belong in the business world. Yet think of the projects that you have worked on that you really threw yourself into, enjoyed and gave your all. It is the passion and motivation that makes the difference.

If our leaders really believe something and show it, we are much more likely to trust them and want to follow them, because it is hard to fake passion. Passion is simply the illumination of something that someone cares about or feels strongly about.

They speak from the heart not just from their intellect

This is linked to passion. People who really care about something, and are truly committed, do not just talk about it at an intellectual level. True passion does not come from the intellect.

The CEO who gives sound rational speeches is much less engaging and much less likely to be trusted than the one who tells stories and speaks about personal experiences. Trusted leaders talk about their feelings as well as their thoughts and ideas. Human beings need to connect at a deeper level if they are to do amazing things. An intellectual understanding is important but is not enough and sometimes is not even necessary.

When Simon Woodroffe went about setting up the Yo Sushi! restaurant chain in London, he had no idea how he was going to do it, whether it would work or how he would get funding and support, but he had an exciting vision and he rallied people around it. A well-written business plan does not have the power of a passionately spoken vision that reveals something of the person's values. People *want* to trust when they can align with values.

They confront people without being confrontational

We trust someone who we can rely on to tell us the truth. Many managers are reluctant to do this because they are afraid that they will not be able to handle someone's reaction, they are afraid of hurting people's feelings, they want to be liked or they simply feel uncomfortable about having that kind of difficult conversation. If we do not know what the leader really thinks then we are forever hedging or second-guessing.

An important part of the leader's integrity is that they say it as it is. Richard Reed of the Innocent Drinks Company told us that people trust him as a leader because 'I won't deviate from harsh reality no matter how bad the news is'. He says that the management team are close friends and that helps. 'We know each other inside out and we can be painfully honest with each other. ... We don't hide behind anything, we know each other's strengths and flaws and we are totally open and honest.'

They don't mind admitting they don't know

Trusted leaders do not mind talking about their vulnerabilities. And they are ready to admit when they are wrong.

We tend to be suspicious of people who act as though they are right all the time, who think they know all the answers and who will not admit when they get it wrong. It is logical to conclude that people who think they are right all the time cannot be trusted because they delude themselves as well as others.

Many leaders believe that they should have all the answers and that it is a sign of weakness if they do not. It is hard for them to admit they do not know. The important thing for leaders is that they know what they want to achieve, they have a vision. They cannot possibly know enough about everything that is needed to achieve that vision. They may sometimes make mistakes or get it wrong. The following story, which was adapted from a real-life situation, shows the positive effects of being willing to admit you have got it wrong and change course.[3]

M4 is a successful start-up company. Founded by a software designer called Peter Parsons and a businesswoman called Melissa Thorpe, in three years it has grown to an 80-person outfit. It has a good income from software development contracts with a handful of industry leaders around the world. Now M4 wants to raise capital, in an initial public offering (IPO) of its shares. The company wants the money in order to produce its own software packages for general marketing. Following this fundraising, it hopes to attract lots more talented technical staff, to go on working for large customers and to release its own products as soon as they are ready for the market.

Melissa Thorpe, the CEO, has a reputation in the industry as tough, decisive and hard driving. She holds monthly meetings of all staff at which she talks about the things – both good and bad – that have happened since the last meeting. Peter Parsons, the technical director, reports on M4's various projects. When a contract is secured, there is a noisy cheer. When one is lost there is a sober discussion on what went wrong. Key decisions like going public are reviewed at some length. Policy developments are reported.

At one of the monthly meetings, Melissa announced her intention to pay bonuses to staff responsible for getting important contracts. 'These contracts are vital for our future cashflow,' she declared, 'and those who win them deserve recognition for this.'

'Wait a minute,' said a young software writer. 'It's our work that enables these deals to take place. It's the job of salespeople to sell, so why should they get special rewards just for doing their job? We don't.'

Melissa responded that in this industry salespeople expected bonuses. But that argument was not accepted.

'M4 is not a typical company. This is a place where everyone works together. Don't destroy that by giving special treatment to one group of people.'

Melissa realised she had made a mistake. Her first reaction was to tough it out, because she did not want to demoralise the sales staff. Nor did she want to admit that she had not properly thought her policy through. But after a moment she said: 'OK. I'm probably wrong. Maybe any bonuses should be for everyone.'

This became a famous moment in M4's history, and it was told to people who joined the company after the event, as an example of the company's culture. It was clear that the CEO would listen to a sound argument and that company communication goes both ways.

They have integrity

Integrity means being honest, keeping confidences, keeping promises and respecting other people's boundaries. Leaders who lack integrity cannot hope to gain the trust of their staff. People will always be wary and careful about what they say.

They use power positively

They are interested in power only because having it will enable them to do more of the right thing, not as a way of supporting their own ego. They use power not to dominate, but for productive reasons. We have all met managers for whom power is a perk. They love wielding it over others and use it to boost their own egos, not to further any positive aim.

LEAVING A LEGACY

For anyone who is a leader and is looking for ways to increase their 'trust quotient', the list above may seem an intimidating and impossibly long list of 'to-dos'.

Another, more simple way of thinking about how to become a trusted leader is to think about what legacy you want to leave. Sadly, many business leaders today seem not to be particularly interested in leaving anything. They are more interested in the financial package that they can walk away with, as evidenced by the number of corporate scandals in recent years.

As for politicians, it is sometimes even harder to discern the legacy that they are seeking to leave. One would hope it would be something like making their country and the world a better and more prosperous world to live in. However, that appears not to be the case as Jim Collins argues:

> My hypothesis is that there are two categories of people: those who do not have the seed of Level 5 [leadership] and those who do. The first category consists of people who could never in a million years bring themselves to subjugate their egoistic needs to the greater ambition of building something larger and more lasting than themselves. For these people, work will be first and foremost about what they *get* – fame, fortune, adulation, power, whatever – not what they *build,* create, and contribute.

If a leader wants to leave a legacy of some greater good, wants to leave something behind that lasts long into the future, to create something that makes a difference, something to be proud of, then people are likely to trust him or her. They are likely to overlook any mistakes or small transgressions because they know that *their leader's intention is positive.*

71

A TALE OF A TRUSTED LEADER

In writing this book, we came across some exceptional leaders. We found these people to be understated and free of egotism. We were struck by their willingness to admit mistakes and to learn. It was refreshing to hear them speak very honestly and openly about their lives and work. It was easy to see how they had become the trusted leaders that they were.

Gerard Fairtlough, founder and CEO of the biotechnology company Celltech, is one of these people. This is the story of the appointment of his successor.

Gerard emphasised that you should do everything that you can to attract the very best people to an organisation and that you should develop their talents to the full. When the time came to find a successor to his position of CEO at Celltech, he was determined not to make the classic mistake of the founder who cannot let go. So he was delighted to have at his side an apparently ideal replacement: his current deputy. This person (called Peter for the purposes of this story) was an excellent salesman, with whom Gerard got on well. He was very keen to take over from Gerard. However, the non-executive chairman, a man with whom Gerard had never had a particularly close relationship, was non-committal about the idea. The board decided that Peter would not get the job and that they would recruit externally, and Peter resigned. Gerard was asked to stay on as a non-executive director but, in light of what had happened, he refused. His retirement date grew near and no replacement had been found. Things looked bleak for Celltech. Then, a senior person from the pharmaceutical industry expressed an interest. The board had little choice but to agree to his appointment, but fortunately the new CEO did a fantastic job. Gerard said that he now knows, more than a decade later, that it was a mistake to get involved in the succession. He recognises that in trying to choose his successor he was hanging on to his creation. He concealed from himself that he didn't want to let go of his baby.

This kind of humility, self-insight and ability to learn is the stuff that trusted leaders are made of.

A Fresh Perspective

Chris Robinson, Chief Executive, CHASE Children's Hospice Service

I was homeless as a child in London. My Mum, my sister and I had to stay in a homeless hostel near Marble Arch but my Dad was not allowed to stay at the same place. I can remember him visiting us. We were not there that long but we never forgot it.

However, I always say, I had a very privileged childhood. I was loved and told I was loved every day; I was given confidence and attention. We were just poor at that time in material terms. I was also taught the difference between right and wrong and taught not to lie.

I never tell a lie.

It has not always been that way! If I look back over my nearly 50 years I can remember some really big lies. However, in more recent years, I gradually came home to the basic truths I had been taught as a child. For me, as it happens, my route back to the truth was through Buddhism but the vehicle is not so important as the destination.

Through my working life – from working on the docks on the Isle of Dogs, through putting myself through universities (B.A. Hons., M.Sc. Econ., also currently doing a part-time Ph.D. in Buddhist Studies), to economic research for the European parliament, through being a full-time Trade Union official (at 23) to standing for Parliament (at 29), to management and financial consultancy, to full-time football coaching here and abroad, to football management (Cheltenham Town amongst others), and finally to charity management – I have had all sorts of bosses.

On my first day at work on the docks my boss, the Wharf boss – who was also my Dad – threw someone over the wall into the Thames! I can remember then at sixteen thinking 'Well, that's not my style!' But I also learned that he was respected more because he was fair – a 'straight' man.

Now it seems to me that unless you tell the truth yourself then how can you expect to be trusted? And if you cannot be trusted how can you inspire trust? I cannot in practice divide personal trust and honesty from that in a corporate setting. I don't think you can split yourself in two and have one 'real' personality and reflect another different one to your working colleagues – or not for long, anyway.

And how do you present this 'self', this 'personality'? By forgetting it.

If you stick to some basic guidelines then the rest will follow. You do not have to worry about what others might think of you or how you appear to others. OK, in a corporate sense, you might need to think about how you communicate and present your decisions and approaches. But if you lose the 'ego', lose the big worry about how you might look, then the guidelines will shine through.

How you are everyday, with those closest to you, is what matters first.

At home (and I have seven children!) we have five 'house rules' stuck up on our kitchen wall. They are:

1.   No killing anything.
2.   No getting angry.
3.   No blaming others.
4.   No stealing.
5.   No lying.

That's a hard enough standard. But if we try and stick to that we reckon we won't be far wrong.

So, 'no stealing'? Well, last week I was in a fine hotel in Edinburgh and we had had a reception there the night before and also had about 20 people staying. One of my team went to get the bill and it was £400. It should have been about £2000! Obviously a mistake had been made. "What shall we do?' She sighed and handed me the bill. 'Need I ask?' she said. She knew what I would say. We paid our bill. Not taking what is not given is what this is all about, too.

And 'no lying'? What about if someone has done really well on a campaign but it has not produced the goods. I might say 'You worked really hard, well done', but I will not say 'It worked'. In most situations there is a positive approach. We do not need to lie.

So, now as Chief Executive of a children's hospice charity which is a £2.5m p.a. business with 70 employees, 200 regular volunteers supporting 160 families with life-limited children, I see no reason to change or modify my belief in personal honesty. Lies make it harder, eventually.

Now, as I have said, I am not saying I am any sort of saint. Far from it. I have lied and cheated along the way big time. I've been married three times, too, so I've seen some promises come and go! Telling lies can become a way of life.

But not now. I've learned it does not help. So I stopped.

Just like with drinking, as it happens. I was never a big drinker but I would have the occasional beer or glass of wine. Then I got to thinking how, through my life, I have never met anyone who was a nicer person for having a drink. So I stopped.

As I say to my kids, I can see only two advantages to growing older. One is your car insurance gets cheaper. The other is you get a chance to learn, or more accurately, many chances to learn. It would be such a waste if we did not put our lessons to good use, wouldn't it?

I'm not bothered if a belief in not telling lies is old fashioned or new fangled or whatever. That does not matter. I do know that 'trust' is built on truth. Truth must be a personal truth at its heart.

It starts at home. For us, in the kitchen, where that battered and breakfast-splattered handwritten sign still flutters.

In the next chapter, we consider the issues faced by organisations, and the significance of trust for them. Efficiency, profitability, risk, innovation and learning are all affected by trust. We explore why it is so important to these issues and how the principles of trust may be applied to increase organisational success and profitability.

6   Trust matters in business

If trust could be bottled and sold it would be in huge demand by business leaders.

In this chapter, we look at some of the core issues that organisations face, and the relevance of trust to these issues. The issues are efficiency, profitability, risk, innovation and learning. We explore why trust is central to them and how the principles of trust may be applied in order to increase organisational success and profitability.

The issues we address apply equally to public sector organisations and the world of politics. Their measures of success are not financial, but the same principles for creating the conditions of success apply in these fields as in the business world.

TRUST AND THE BOTTOM LINE

Nearly all the business people we have spoken to, while writing this book, say they believe that there is a link between a culture of trust and business success, including profitability. Proving it is another matter. Most say they cannot prove 'cause and effect' but this does not stop them believing it and acting as if it is true. Richard Reed of the Innocent Drinks Company said: 'I have no doubt that there is a connection between trust and profitability. I believe it, but good luck trying to prove it'.

In organisational life we get nervous if we cannot prove something. We want 'scientific evidence' that what we are doing is working or is worthwhile. We talk of accountability as the reason for needing to measure and validate. Of course, that is often true and laudable. However, it

> 'The obsession with measurement is the problem. There is something we can use instead of measurement: judgement. Some of the most important things in the world cannot be measured'. (Professor Henry Mintzberg)

seems to have gone too far now. We will often not move without proof because we are frightened and insecure. Frightened that if we get it wrong our bosses will find out, we will lose our jobs, the share price will drop and that we might lose money or public support. The truth is that all of those things can go wrong even if the measurements prove our case, because people are usually smarter than we give them credit for and know what should be happening, even if the figures say something else. Take the measures that are applied to crime. Because it makes good newspaper headlines, governments like to report the number of criminals caught, the number of years they are sentenced to for various crimes and the amounts of money invested in prisons. This might make for comforting headlines in the tabloid press but what would really make a difference is to invest in the type of rehabilitation programmes that are being shown to work. But that would mean reporting small numbers initially and it might also mean investing in trials of new approaches that cannot yet be statistically proven to be effective. So they stick with the old measures.

This obsession with using statistics to justify or 'sell' a particular course of action is strong and unrelenting in organisational life. In some organisations the bureaucratic processes are such that judgement of any kind is driven out; rules and procedures are believed to be the way of accountable and responsible management.

Even in organisations with little bureaucracy, managers who are insecure and afraid of trusting their own or others' judgements use the measurement argument as something to hide behind.

In a speech to the US Academy of Management in 2003, Professor Henry Mintzberg said: 'The obsession with measurement is the problem. There is something we can use instead of measurement: judgement. Some of the most important things in the world cannot be measured. Remember McNamara's body counts in Vietnam?'

If you get into arguments about issues that cannot be measured in business then you are never going to win. Unless managers are persuasive or charismatic enough, they usually end sloping away from statistics-free presentations with their tails between their legs!

I recall a conversation that I had with a senior executive in a major oil company. He was responsible for a region of the world that was well away, in distance and in culture, from the corporate centre. He told me that he had wanted to invest in training in a number of different cultural and management issues for his workers, to help them to understand one another and build relationships. He had been required to put together a business case for this investment. He did this and it was approved. Once the training had been done he was besieged by requests from head office asking for proof that the investment had been worthwhile. 'They wanted numbers and they wanted proof of return on investment.' He said he could not prove it but he knew it had made a difference as he sensed a different quality of understanding and dialogue among his people. They did not want to hear that. It was 'too flaky'. He was incensed by this attitude. He said that the people who were checking up on him had no understanding, insight or real interest in the issues and problems he faced. They did not have faith that he knew what was needed and that if he said it was worth the investment then it was. So, to circumvent their interference, he invented some statistics about what difference the training had made. He sent these figures in and heard no more. He said he would not have been surprised if his colleagues at head office had never even looked at them!

Some of the most important things cannot be measured

In life, how do we measure love, fun, enjoyment, happiness? We usually know when we have those things but it is impossible to create measures of relativity or success. Yet these are some of the most important human experiences.

Why do we think it should be any different in organisations and business?

In organisational life, how do we measure loyalty, commitment, passion, creativity, morale and the satisfaction of our employees and customers? These are some of the most important aspects of any organisation's life and are certainly crucial to its success.

There are some quantitative measures that we can put into place but they never give the whole picture; indeed, they probably miss the most important parts. You can measure sales, profits, margins and growth, but none of those figures will give you any information about the quality of the customer experience – why they love certain aspects of your products or service and why they hate others. Nor will they tell you why people love to work for you and what really motivates them to do the best job they possibly can. In fact, customers and employees are often not consciously aware of why exactly something motivates them (to do an outstanding job in the case of the employee, or buy more of your services in the case of a customer). How can you measure something that even your customers are unaware of?

We are not arguing that quantitative measures are unimportant, just that they cannot cover everything and that they sometimes show only a tiny, relatively inconsequential, part of the picture. Yet because we can produce reams of reports and statistics, we kid ourselves that we are in control of our business, that our investment appraisals are sound and that we can justify our actions to the shareholders and investors.

Businesses are undoubtedly, to a greater or lesser extent, driven by a desire to keep the analysts happy. However, analysts tend to be looking at a short time horizon. They are interested in short-term growth and some are undoubtedly influenced greatly by the likely size of this year's bonus in their pay packet. Indeed, many CEOs have the same focus.

It is true that in recent years analysts and investors have started to pay more attention in their investment appraisals to the quality of the leadership and the teams that are running businesses. But, again, they tend to only look at data that is reasonably quantifiable and easy to gather, such as experience and track record, career history and skill sets. This information tells you nothing of the quality and effectiveness of the leadership. Ironically, in the end, it is those two variables that make the difference. The ability of the leader to create an organisation and culture that delivers results is critical to success.

There are many organisations that believe their own spin. The executive teams spend time analysing their growth curves, margins, cost savings and new customer acquisition figures and satisfy themselves (and their stakeholders) that they are doing well and delivering value. Few ask themselves how much better they could be doing and seriously address that question, except by increasing targets.

Business leaders are good at self-congratulation and hyping of any successes they have achieved. Few organisations encourage people to declare the gaps in their achievement and find creative ways of doing better than anyone would think possible; most reward those who are extremely good at self-marketing.

David Whyte, a poet who works as a consultant in large American corporations, asks executives: 'What are the courageous conversations that you are not having here?' He encourages them to be brave and to speak about the really difficult matters. He believes that it is these conversations that lead people to address the issues that are holding companies back. The kinds of issues that people talk about in their 'courageous conversations' are ones that inhibit productive relationships, that stifle honesty and truth-telling, that leave people feeling afraid to take risks and be creative and, ultimately, have people use only a very small amount of potential in their work.

In his book *The Heart Aroused* David Whyte recounts the story of a friend who had a powerful experience of being unable to have a much-needed courageous conversation:

> A man I know finds himself in a meeting room at the very edge of speech; he is approaching his moment of reckoning and is looking for support from his fellow executives around the table. Strangely, at this moment, no one will look at him. The CEO is pacing up and down on the slate gray carpet. He has asked, in no uncertain terms, for their opinion of the plan he wants to put through. 'I want to know what you all think about this' he demands, *'on a scale of one to ten.'*
>
> The CEO is testy; he makes it plain he wants everyone to say *'ten,'* and damn whether they mean it or not. He is just plain tired, after all this time, of people resisting his ideas on the matter. He glares at them, he wants compliance. My friend thinks the plan is terrible and that there is too much riding on this solitary ego; everyone in the company will lose by it. He is sure also, from talk he has heard, that half the other executives in the

room think so too. As they go round the shamefaced table, the voices of those present sound alternatively overconfident, or brittle and edgy. Most say '*ten*', one courageous soul braves a '*nine and a half*' and my friend is the last to go. He reaches his hand toward the flame, opens his palm against the heat, and suddenly falters; against everything he believes, he hears a mouselike faraway voice, his own, say '*ten*.'[1]

Having courageous conversations in organisations usually means taking personal and professional risks. As David Whyte's story shows, people often want to say what they really think but, in the end, the risk to them is too great. But courageous conversations, when they become possible, lead people to a new level of dialogue in organisations. They are able to speak about things that previously they were not. This kind of honesty takes trust. And this is the kind of honesty that certainly leads organisations to avoid doing the wrong things, and also gives them the ability to do great things.

Jim Collins argues that great companies confront the brutal facts relentlessly:

Like Nucor, all the good-to-great companies had a penchant for intense dialogue. Phrases like 'loud debate', 'heated discussions', and 'healthy conflict' peppered the articles and interview transcripts from all the companies. They didn't use discussion as a sham process to let people 'have their say' so that they could 'buy in' to a predetermined decision. The process was more like a heated scientific debate, with people engaged in a search for the best answers.

Do the right thing and the money will follow

I was once working on a project with James, a senior executive whose wisdom I had seriously underestimated. The project was an important one, as it was addressing serious problems that stood in the way of delivering what the customer wanted. There were many managers who were sceptical about what we were trying to do. Some were openly against it. So we did it in a low-key way. We gradually changed things and, slowly, the improvements started to happen. After several months we reached a point where we could start to 'prove' that what we were doing was right and should be supported by all the senior managers. At this point, I started to push James to agree revenue targets so that we could demonstrate in a 'hard' way that this project was adding value. I spent a fair amount of time working on this and talking to him about it. He in the meantime continued to relentlessly support the people who were trying to do things differently for the customer. Eventually, after another one of my pleas to him to set stretch targets so we could prove our case he gently turned to me and said 'Sally, if we continue to do the right things the revenue will follow'. Indeed it did. We both put our energy into doing the job. We spent minimal time measuring, monitoring and justifying.

We are not saying that measurement and focus on profit is wrong. But too many companies focus on it to the detriment of attending to other things that drive profit, like employee and customer satisfaction.

Once again, the words of Richard Reed from the Innocent Drinks Company come to mind: 'We don't want to please our customers we aim to infatuate them. We are doing what we care about. It's a cause not a profit line.'

Clearly both these examples involve people doing something that they really care about and feel is right irrespective of resistance. The people involved have good relationships with each other: they can speak up and say what they think. That is not possible, without trust.

Another way of looking at the question of whether there is a relationship between trust and profitability is to ask how much more profitable a company could be if it had a culture of trust. Imagine what a very trusting culture would mean:

- Senior management could question and challenge the board and vice versa in a spirit of wanting to find the right solution, not in a spirit of wanting to appear to be in control.
- Employees could tell management exactly how things are, not what they want to hear.
- People could say what is on their minds, speak openly about their concerns and seek advice and guidance from others.
- People would be able to take the risk to suggest and do new things.
- People would not have to hide their mistakes.
- People could tell others when they feel they are doing the wrong thing or going in the wrong direction.
- No gossip and backstabbing.
- No second-guessing and trying to anticipate what the boss wants you to do.
- No jockeying for position and time wasted on self-promotion.

This would be likely to lead to:

- better-informed decisions on strategic direction, operational issues and investment
- less time wasted
- people focusing on the right thing instead of the things that might not be right but that no one dare speak up against
- identifying problems and solving them early
- more time and energy spent on the customers and less on managing the internal politics
- better motivated, confident employees
- better PR, as people would not be complaining to their family and friends about the company

- a workforce of people who are motivated to do a good job rather than being motivated to increase their personal power base.

It seems hard to imagine that a culture of trust, with the benefits that it yields, would not lead to a more successful and profitable company. If people are able to discuss issues and problems honestly, it will lead to good business decisions. Add to that a motivated workforce who feel that their voice counts and that they can get on with the job, and it is logical to expect that the result will be a more effective and efficient place of work.

Trust means efficiency

A senior executive in a global corporation told me about two of his colleagues. He was based in New York, one colleague was in London and the other in Sydney. He said that over time he had built a good relationship with the one in Sydney. They often had different views on issues but they talked openly and honestly and always worked things out. He said he felt that each of them genuinely wanted to support the other and they would help each other out where possible. The London-based colleague was very pleasant, always offering to support him but quite often not delivering. It was not that he was unpleasant; it was rather that he often said he would do things and just never did. One particular global project relied on the three of them working closely together to tight time-scales. They spent a long time talking about what exactly needed to be done, how they would get it done and they agreed a timetable. The man in London did not deliver. The executive told me that he had always been able to work so much more efficiently with the person in Sydney because they would talk ideas through, hammer things out and then get on and get the job done. With the one in London, however, he found that he had to spend a lot of time informally 'contracting', putting things in writing and finding subtle ways of getting others involved as 'insurance policies'. It was hugely inefficient, and, as was the case with the big project, often not very successful.

When people trust one another to keep their commitments at work they discuss what needs to be done, agree who will do what, commit to when they will do it – and then get on and do it. When they do not trust each other they do the same, but it takes longer because they have to go into more detail and be very specific about 'contracting', whether formally or informally. It takes longer and is a much less efficient way of doing business. In this scenario, commitments are fulfilled often because of the contractual obligation, not because of the personal commitment.

Trust and risk

Most big companies now write down what behaviours they want people to display. They often label these behaviours 'competencies'. There can be anything up to 20 competencies on a company's list, and 'risk-taking' is often one of them.

Why would they want people to take risks and what do they mean by risk-taking? They want people to try out new ways of doing things, to challenge the received wisdom in the company; sometimes they say they want people to challenge management. Their hope is that people will help the company to be more profitable or more competitive by doing things in ways that have previously not been thought of.

Few companies actually give much thought to what happens in their culture when someone tries to take a risk. Unless there is an environment that really does enable people to push the boundaries, people are not going to feel safe enough to do it.

When an employee suggests to a colleague or boss that something could be done in a different way, there are usually several hurdles to jump.

- *Hurdle one.* A closed-minded or defensive person who does not want to listen.
- *Hurdle two.* Even if the boss is prepared to listen, the innovator will have to argue a strong case. New ideas have usually got to have a stronger rationale than something that has been in place for years, even if that something doesn't make a lot of sense.
- *Hurdle three.* The boss's boss. Once you have got through the boss, you have to persuade his or her boss. This person will probably want to have an input.
- *Hurdle four.* A strong business case. At each stage of 'approval', a good business case will probably be needed.

Without an assumption that people can be trusted to do their job and do not need to be checked up on, then the obstacles become tougher. Even the most enthusiastic person with a real belief in a fantastic new idea can lose the will to live in the process of jumping all these hurdles.

When trust is present these hurdles take on a different meaning. The big difference is that someone who wants to take that much-coveted *risk* is questioned with a spirit of inquiry and a genuine desire to find out instead of with suspicion.

Trust and innovation

The UK-based innovation company *?What If!* teaches its clients how to make their organisations more innovative. Their processes challenge people to see things differently by stepping out of their comfort zone and risking saying something that may seem not to make sense. They talk about two key, but separate, processes that are needed for innovation. One is idea building, where people come up with the ideas, build on them and nurture them; the other is where these well-formed ideas are subject to analysis.

Companies that struggle to be innovative often do so because ideas get trampled in their infancy by the big boots of judgement and analysis.

Having the right kind of processes for idea generation and innovation is important, but processes are not enough. Innovative organisations are so because they also have an environment and culture that support and foster innovation. It is flogging the same old point to say that a culture of trust enables people to step out, take risks and come up with ideas that they are passionate about. It is true, though, and cannot be overstated.

Javier Bajer, Chief Executive of The Talent Foundation, says:

> At the Talent Foundation we had a strong 'gut feeling'. A strong sense that, after working with so many senior executives in large and small, public and private organisations, there was no real 'magic formula' for doing innovation. Instead, we found it was the way they were *being* about it.[2]

The Foundation had done their own research: they had looked at work done by leading academics and successful innovators around the world, and they pulled all of this together in a paper in which they identified five catalysts for innovation. The catalysts are a set of characteristics that they found in successful innovators. They are:

- *Consciousness.* Each person knows the goals of the organisation and believes he or she can play a part in achieving them.
- *Multiplicity.* Teams and groups contain a wide and creative mix of skills, experiences, backgrounds and ideas.
- *Connectivity.* Relationships are strong and trusting and are actively encouraged within and across teams and functions.
- *Accessibility.* Doors and minds are open; everyone in the organisation has access to resources, time and decision makers.
- *Consistency.* Commitment to innovation runs right through the organisation and is built into processes and leadership styles.

The notion that a strong informal network can help to facilitate innovation is one that some companies have been inspired by. If people get to know one another and are encouraged to do so, then trust develops. What is more, companies who realise this understand that it is what knowledge management really means. Systems are important but it is in the connections between people that knowledge is really exchanged in a way that is relevant to them and to the issues they are concerned with at that time.

Laurence Prusak, executive director of the IBM Institute for Knowledge Management, and Dan Cohen, writer and consultant, advise companies to

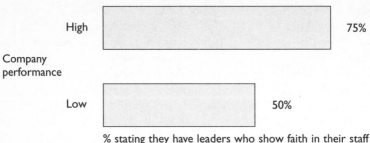

Figure 6.1 Top-performing companies have leaders who show faith and trust in their staff

Source: The Talent Foundation.

invest in what they call 'social capital' by giving people time and space to bond with each other, facilitating personal conversations and fostering durable networks. They believe that companies can enable connections at work, creating environments where people know and trust one another by making a commitment to retention and promoting from within.[3]

The Talent Foundation found that organisations with leaders who have faith in their staff, who allow ambiguity and provide space for creativity, tend to perform better. According to research undertaken by the Foundation:

> The ideal environment for innovation is made up of people who are conscious of overall company strategies and goals; support multiplicity through a broad and diverse set of skills and perspectives and tolerance of new ideas; are part of a web of interconnected relationships based on trust in which information flows freely; are supportive of each other and provide freedom and space for innovation, as well as access to time, management and decision makers; and seek to sustain innovation through consistency of the HR processes, leadership and tools.

Pfizer is a leading pharmaceutical company. It has gained its leading position by being innovative. Jennifer Perry, Corporate Public Relations Manager, says: 'If you trust people and give them responsibilities, they react well.'

When Pfizer moved their UK commercial headquarters to a site closer to London, so that it could increase capacity and attract talent, they involved all of their employees in the process. They set up steering committees and focus groups. These groups made recommendations for the policy on office accommodation, dress code and other issues. The new building looks more like a contemporary hotel than an office block. The structure was built so that people bump into each other and have a chance to network. Richard Crow, Director of Projects, says:

Pfizer is developing an environment that will enable people and encourage creativity. We attract and retain the best people and treat colleagues as mature adults who know what needs doing. At Pfizer we believe in measuring the output not the input and providing staff with more flexibility on all fronts to reach their potential in an innovative and creative environment. The performance of our business speaks for itself and indicates that this approach really works.

Trust and learning

During the summer, my nine-year-old nephew, Keaton, was playing golf on the lawn at the back of my apartment block. My neighbour Ken came out and saw him. His first words were to ask him not to hit the ball in the direction of the apartments in case he broke a window. You could have forgiven Keaton if he had thought that here was a man coming out to scold him. He had only met Ken a couple of times, so did not know what this person was like. Ken started to chat and complimented Keaton on his stance. He showed a real interest and started to encourage Keaton as he made some really good swings. As I watched, this turned into a small coaching session. Keaton accepted Ken's coaching and seemed to enjoy his interest. What Ken had done in that half hour was to demonstrate to Keaton that he was on his side and that he was interested in him and his golf playing. He had started to build Keaton's trust and he treated him with respect and interest. Ideal conditions for learning.

Imagine if Ken had done what I had seen others before him do. Imagine if he commented on what Keaton was doing wrong, if he criticised his swing when he hit the ball, if he stood at a distance throwing clever observations his way and even (and I saw someone do this once) if he had snatched the club out of his hand to demonstrate 'how it should be done'. This approach would have signalled to Keaton that Ken was a man who was more interested in showing off his own knowledge and skills than in helping and encouraging a keen young boy with his.

Trust is such an important condition for learning. People have to feel sure that the teacher, coach or trainer genuinely has their interests at heart and is on their agenda not their own.

Tom Bentley in his book *Learning Beyond the Classroom* says:

> Finally, the bedrock of an effective learning relationship is trust. Trust, the willingness to believe that people will act in good faith and honour their commitments, is what underpins the development of fair, cohesive communities and prosperous, dynamic economies. In a learning relationship, trust cements and sustains the norms of collaboration – communication, shared experience, common purpose and mutual respect. As it grows it eliminates the need for caution; strong, secure ties to parents among

young children permit them to experiment more at the boundaries of their experience, to interact with new people and test out unfamiliar surroundings. Trust strengthens our capacity to take purposeful risks, deviating from established patterns or disseminating from the common view for the sake of achieving shared goals more effectively. Detailed and petty rules can be abandoned as the bonds of trust are strengthened, between individuals, and within and across groups of learners. Trust is reflected in the depth of common knowledge and experience, the intimacy and extent of mutual confidence between learners.[4]

Learning is such a fundamental capability of organisations in today's complex and ever-changing world. To be able to learn even the most basic of new skills people have to feel that they won't be laughed at if they get it wrong. They need to be confident that it is fine for them to get it wrong at first and that they will have the support they need until they get to a stage where they feel competent.

The organisations that create a climate where real learning and experimentation can take place are the most adaptable. They are the ones that are versatile and quick enough to be able to change in response to market and customer demands. The value of this cannot be overstated. Trust is at the core of what it takes to get there.

7   Building customer trust

Corporate values are a genuine competitive advantage ... an enduring factor amid so many changes in product and service.   (Rosabeth Moss Kanter)

Trust is a business issue that fundamentally affects relationships with current and potential customers. It underpins such issues as innovation, benefiting and adding value for customers, enhancing loyalty, winning new business, building the long-term value of the business (and especially the brand) and serving customers. Without trust, all of these issues become much, much harder to achieve – if they can be achieved at all. Yet inspiring trust should not be a difficult issue; it simply requires us to live certain values that are often lacking in the commercial world. They are openness, honesty, consistency and a real regard for the needs of others.

This chapter explores ways in which organisations can inspire the trust of their customers and create long-lasting, mutually beneficial relationships.

WHY TRUST IS IMPORTANT FOR CUSTOMERS

Meeting the challenges of changing markets

Relationships based on trust are essential for meeting the challenges of changing markets. In a fast-moving, highly competitive and increasingly global environment, businesses need to develop and change if they are to remain profitable and successful. Building a firm base of trust and confidence in brands, products and service is the key to success in the three dominant forms of rivalry for customers: turning potential customers into actual ones, capturing them from rivals and competing for sales to shared customers.

The organisations that are successful at this are good at understanding customers' needs and consistently meeting them.

Increasing customer loyalty and revenues

This is a story that illustrates the profound benefit of seeking to understand each customer, gaining deep insight into individual needs and then fulfilling them. It illustrates the point that, if you do the right thing and offer real value to customers, the revenue will follow.

For the sake of commercial confidentiality we will call the company ABC Services and their customers Star Computers.

A young salesperson, Anna, had a call from Star Computers, explaining that they were looking to give a provider a large piece of global business, but before they got to the tendering stage they wanted to get initial ideas from all the prospective bidders. Anna was excited by this but knew that in order to get some great ideas she would have to go around speaking to colleagues in other parts of the business. She would need to ask them to spend some of their time helping her to come up with ideas that at worst might be stolen by the client, at best would win them much more business than they had got in the previous years. The thought that some of her colleagues would probably be less than enthusiastic about spending time on something that might not even contribute to their business (and therefore their own personal commission) immediately dampened her enthusiasm, and she started to wonder whether she should even bother. By chance she bumped into a colleague, Alex, at the coffee machine and told her about the opportunity. Alex was one of those very positive people who cared passionately about delighting the customer. She suggested emailing a senior person who had recently told them to 'let him know if there is anything I can do to help' and asking him to spend an hour in an ideas session with her. By the end of the conversation they decided it was probably a good idea to also invite the sales people from all other departments to see who was interested enough to come and help. Anna did this and six people showed up the following day, including the senior person who had cleared his diary to help. They had a great session in terms of the quality of the ideas that came out and also in terms of the passion and commitment it inspired. They had many great ideas, including ones that they could not deliver for the client but that other partners would be able to. They presented all of the ideas to the client, effectively providing them with 'free' consultancy and, unsurprisingly, they won the business. The client was not only impressed by the quality of the ideas that ABC services proposed but also by their taking the time to really understand their needs and create a solution that went beyond ABC's own capability. Star said that they had never encountered such open-mindedness and commitment before. The effect of this additional effort, which was not done just to get more money out of the client, had a profound effect on customer loyalty and trust.

This case speaks for itself. It is about commitment to doing whatever is possible for the client. It is also a big lesson in the power of doing a great job because you care about the client, not just because you are driving towards revenue. Even if Star Computers had not liked the ideas, the effort that ABC services made would have impressed them and had a positive effect on the relationship, the benefits of which are impossible to quantify but are clearly significant. This route is undoubtedly more effective than any marketing or PR campaign in building clients' trust and loyalty. They are unlikely to forget this experience in a hurry.

The other lesson in this is the impact of a senior manager's willingness to give high priority to this junior salesperson's request to help a customer. This kind of response has a strong and lasting effect. Anna now has a senior person who she knows is willing to practise what he preaches and really can be relied upon to give support. The motivating effect of this kind of act should not be underestimated; and, customers do know whether they are dealing with motivated or demotivated sales people. Research supports the notion that there is a direct link between employee satisfaction and customer satisfaction. This is a case in point.

TRUST BUILDS LOYALTY

Consider these quotations, made by people who understand customers and business:

> PR cannot overcome things that should have been done. (Harold Burson)

> Brands have always been about the relationship between product and user. (Shelly Lazarus)

> People do not buy much from a man who fails to command their respect. (William Wrigley)

> If someone thinks they are being mistreated by us, they won't tell five people, they'll tell 5,000. (Jeff Bezos)

Customer loyalty is a big issue for business. It costs more to acquire a new customer than it does to keep an existing one. Businesses ultimately want to get and keep customers, because those that manage to retain them over the long term have a competitive advantage. This is why loyalty programmes have become such an important part of many business strategies of many organisations, including airlines, retailers and credit card companies. It is a smart strategy. But loyalty is not just about giving customers financial incentives (money-off vouchers, discount fares) or 'bells and whistles' (extra services, free offers); it is about demonstrating that you deserve their loyalty in the service you give and the way you respond to them.

There are many examples of how companies have built customer loyalty, some in innovative ways.

BUILDING CUSTOMERS' LOYALTY: LESSONS FROM THE TRUSTED

Building and maintaining customer loyalty is not possible unless customers trust the brand and its products. Here are some examples of companies that have built customer trust and loyalty. In one case the company recovered that trust after having almost lost it in such a big way that it could have not only put them out of business but damaged the entire pharmaceutical industry.

The host with the most: Ritz-Carlton

By applying information technology and training all of its staff, the Ritz-Carlton hotel chain has developed into one of the most successful luxury hotel groups, providing customers with a highly personalised service. The Ritz strategy is quite simple and not at all uncommon: to differentiate itself from its competitors by offering a service that is reliable (or trusted) and distinctive, at a competitive price.

The approach adopted by Ritz (which won the company a prestigious Baldridge Award for total quality) succeeded by emphasising several key principles, all of which were underpinned by a blend of effective leadership and the successful management and application of technology. First, a vision of an efficient, personalised service was formed, and the individual commitment of employees to realising this vision and providing a quality service was then developed. IT systems were standardised throughout the business, and an organisational culture was developed that emphasised the need to capture and disseminate useful information about each individual customer, re-using information and knowledge gained about internal processes as well as customers' wants. This highlighted the general need to listen to the market, as well as the specific requirement to swiftly focus people, information and processes on delivering the benefits of a highly customised and attentive service.

The current challenges for the business are to operate its hotels so that they are error-free, and also to retain all of its customers through a precision marketing strategy. To achieve this, Ritz-Carlton has spent years accumulating in-depth knowledge about its work processes and has assiduously combined technology with individual skills and innovation. In practice, this means it tracks individual customer preferences, using several types of information systems to collect, store and disseminate information only when needed. At each hotel, for instance, employees observe guests, record their preferences and store the data on a company-wide information network. This enables other employees to re-use the information and provide the most personalised service available, leveraging their contact with the customer to shut out competitors. When customers check in they receive the room and location they prefer, and throughout their stay Ritz-Carlton supervisors scrutinise relevant details for each customer so that they can personalise the hotel's service, providing extra pillows, favourite beverages, preferred newspapers and so forth.

The Ritz-Carlton approach is a stunning example of the power of *mass customisation*: the ability to deliver rapidly, efficiently and profitably a range of products and services that satisfy individual customers.

IKEA shelve their universal approach

Since its establishment in Sweden in the 1940s, IKEA has grown into a global organisation selling products that are typically Swedish. The organisation sees itself as existing in – and as part of – the national cultures of countries as diverse as Russia and Kuwait, Canada and Malaysia. Specific national websites demonstrate the individuality of the dispersed business units, yet the organisation emphasises that it is no accident that the IKEA logo is blue and yellow, as these are the colours of the Swedish flag. The products are both intrinsically Swedish and bespoke to the markets in which they are delivered. They are both generic and particular.

Building upon its success in its home market, IKEA expanded rapidly across Europe during the 1970s and 1980s. They sold the same products in the same way, and broke some key principles of retailing. Some of these rules are now broken universally; companies no longer tell the customer that 'we flat pack our products because it is easier and cheaper for *us* to transport and store them', for example, since that seems to ignore the rule of 'putting the customer first'.

When IKEA expanded into North American markets in the 1980s, they discovered that there was no single formula for selling universal products across the global market place. In contrast to their experiences in Europe, the organisation's new stores in North America did not become rapidly profitable. IKEA learned the hard way that the emergence of global markets and acceptance of ideas and concepts across cultures is not a *carte blanche* for the delivery of universal solutions.

In North America, IKEA realised that it had to blend its traditional Swedish design and low-cost offerings with context-specific responses to customer needs and wishes. For example, it changed its furniture range to include chests of drawers with deeper drawers in the USA market, to accommodate more knitwear. Further, to better suit customer preferences, king and queen-sized beds were offered, with measurements given in inches rather than centimetres. By 1997, nearly half of IKEA's offerings in the US market were sourced locally, and nearly a third of its total product offerings were designed exclusively for the USA. Similarly, in recently opened branches in Russia, the products shown on the website vary from those advertised for other European countries.

The first lesson for IKEA was that the growth of business across cultures cannot be based on universal solutions. Though we may have become more international and eclectic, we are still very particular and localised in our tastes.

IKEA is not unique in applying this mix of generalisation and localisation to its products and services. For example, in developing the Focus as an international car model, Ford has addressed the failings of its earlier attempts to offer the Escort as a universal product. The model may be the same, but is adapted in details – such as trim and suspension settings – to suit different tastes across markets and different pragmatic needs based upon environmental conditions. Similarly, MTV has moved from being a universal provider of 24-hour music on television, to exploiting differences in local markets. In Europe, it now provides different language stations; this not only allows it to meet local demand, but also to tap into local advertising markets and generate additional revenues locally.

> **Brands are often criticised and, sadly, abused by their managers. This can mask the fact that a brand's value lies in the understanding that customers receive. It is worth recalling the UK research cited earlier, which showed that many consumers would be prepared to pay 30 per cent extra for a new product from a trusted brand than for an unnamed one.**

At a time of business globalisation and the apparent convergence of cultures – with universal brands such as Sony, McDonald's, IKEA and CNN – successful strategies allow for increased variety and differentiation, helping to create the conditions where trust and understanding can develop and thrive. Successful global companies operate with generic competencies and brands, but offer bespoke solutions within particular contexts. Thus they can align with local needs and demands that are largely driven by cultural differences. To successfully deliver these solutions, organisations need to engage with the members of a particular community, understanding tastes and expectations. At a basic level, this understanding can prevent the mistake of trying to sell 'hamburgers' in Islamic countries. At a deeper level, it facilitates productive relationships based on mutual understanding and respect. The key questions for managers selling to customers abroad are:

- How can I understand the values that are held by others?
- How are my own values demonstrated?
- How do we share an understanding of these values?

FedEx (not fed-up) and the value of openness

Based in Memphis, Tennessee, Federal Express or FedEx Corp is a group of companies offering a broad array of transport and supply-chain solutions worldwide. The business has revolutionised the delivery of packages and information, and now more than 200,000 FedEx employees and contractors handle millions of shipments every day.

The FedEx philosophy is to provide customers with more shipping options, adapting their resources to the needs of their markets and customers and shifting resources as needed. Chairman and founder Frederick W. Smith, realised two other points about his business: customers need confidence that their package will arrive on time and they value information about its progress. When customers work with FedEx, they are trusting the firm to deliver its promise. To meet this challenge, the company nurtured a strong, people-oriented culture in which an employee's performance is ultimately what counts. Consistently focused on recruiting and retaining top talent, FedEx is widely recognised for its progressive policies and benefits, as well as its stimulating working environment. The FedEx passion for customer service and openness has delivered impressive results, as shown in Table 7.1.

It is easy to see why customers trust FedEx and opt for it over competitors: its global network serving 212 countries, its technology systems that give customers real-time information and its human network, built on a culture of passion for customer service.

Table 7.1 FedEx service brings impressive growth

Financial year (June–May)	1998	1999	2000	2001	2002
Revenues (US$m)	15,873	16,774	18,257	19,629	20,607
Net earnings (US$m)	503	631	688	584	710
Earnings per share (US$m)	1.67	2.10	2.32	1.99	2.34
Share price (US$, end of year)	44.56	40.90	39.92	51.83	53.95
Market value (US$m, end of year)	13,297	12,296	11,829	15,196	16,087
Return on shareholders' equity (%)	13.5	14.6	14.6	10.9	11.4

Source: Economist Intelligence Unit.

Johnson & Johnson: relinquishing short-term profit to maintain consumer confidence

This is a dramatic, and thankfully rare, example of a company that could have lost its customers' confidence because some of them died as a result of using one of its products. This happened in the early 1980s. The product is now one of the leading brands of painkiller on the American market.

In 1982 McNeil Consumer Products, a subsidiary of Johnson & Johnson, was confronted with a crisis when seven people on Chicago's West Side died mysteriously. Each had ingested an Extra-Strength Tylenol capsule laced with cyanide.

The capsules in question were each found to contain 65 milligrams of cyanide. The amount of cyanide necessary to kill a human is five to seven micrograms, which means that the person who tampered with the pills used 10,000 times more poison than was needed. Dr Thomas Kim, chief of the Northwest Community Hospital at the time of the poisonings, said: 'The victims never had a chance. Death was certain within minutes.'

Johnson & Johnson faced a major challenge to save the integrity of both the product and the corporation as a whole.

The nation was warned about the danger of Tylenol as soon as a connection was made. Police drove through Chicago announcing the warning over loudspeakers, while all three national television networks reported the deaths from the contaminated drug on their evening news broadcasts. A day later, the Food and Drug Administration advised consumers to avoid the Tylenol capsules 'until the series of deaths in the Chicago area can be clarified'.

McNeil Consumer Products established that the tampering had not taken place at either of its plants, even though cyanide was available on the premises. A spokesman for Johnson & Johnson told the media of the company's strict quality control and showed that the poisonings could not have been performed in the plants. Because the cyanide-laced Tylenol had been discovered in shipments from both plants and only in the Chicago area, authorities concluded that any tampering must have occurred once the Tylenol had reached Illinois.

The tainted capsules were from four different manufacturing lots. Evidence suggests that they were taken from different stores over a period of weeks or months. The bottles, some of which had five or fewer cyanide-laced capsules and one of which had ten, were tampered with and then placed back on the shelves of five different stores in the Chicago area. It seems that the person responsible for the deaths spent some hours distributing the bottles.

The publicity about the cyanide-laced capsules immediately caused a nationwide panic. People in cities across the country were admitted to hospitals on suspicion of cyanide poisoning .

After this crisis, Johnson & Johnson was faced with quite a dilemma. It needed to find the best way to deal with the tampering, without destroying the reputation of the company and its most profitable product, Tylenol. Many marketing experts thought that the brand was doomed by the public's doubts about whether it was safe. 'I don't think they can ever sell another product under that name,' advertising guru Jerry Della Femina told the *New York Times* in the first days following the crisis. 'There may be an advertising person who thinks he can solve this and if they find him, I want to hire him, because then I want him to turn our water cooler into a wine cooler.'

Della Femina was wrong in assuming that Tylenol would never sell again. Not only is it still one of the top-selling over-the-counter drugs in the USA, but it took very little time for the product to return to the market.

Johnson & Johnson's top management put customer safety first, before they worried about their company's profit and other financial concerns. There was apparently some heated debate in the boardroom about whether the product should be completely withdrawn or not. Some executives thought that there was no need to do this as they could prove that the tampering only occurred in a small area and so should just withdraw the products from there. However, the CEO decided that withdrawing all products and the resultant financial loss was necessary to demonstrate to their customers that their safety was Johnson & Johnson's prime concern. He reminded them of their corporate business philosophy, which they call 'Our Credo', when determining how to handle the Tylenol situation.

No crisis management plan would have been appropriate to tackle the Tylenol poisonings, because no management could ever imagine or be prepared for a tragedy of this scale. So Johnson & Johnson turned to their credo for help. 'It was the credo that prompted the decisions that enabled us to make the right early decisions that eventually led to the comeback phase,' says David R. Clare, president of the company at the time.

The credo was written in the mid-1940s by Robert Wood Johnson, the company's leader for 50 years. Little did Johnson know he was writing an outstanding public relations plan. He saw business as having responsibilities to society that went beyond the usual sales and profit incentives. In this respect, Foster explained, Johnson outlined his company's responsibilities to 'consumers and medical professionals using its products, employees, the communities where its people work and live, and its stockholders'. Johnson believed that if his company stayed true to these responsibilities, his business would flourish in the long run. He felt that his credo was not only moral, but profitable as well.

As the Tylenol crisis began, and became more serious as the hours went by, the top management turned to that document for guidance. As the credo stressed, it was important for Johnson & Johnson to be responsible in working for the public interest.

The company immediately warned consumers across the nation, via the media, not to consume any type of Tylenol product. Johnson & Johnson, along with stopping the production and advertising of Tylenol, recalled all the capsules from the market: some 31 million bottles with a retail value of more than 100 million dollars.

This was unusual for a large corporation facing a crisis. In many similar cases companies had put financial considerations first, and ended up doing more damage to their reputations than if they had immediately taken responsibility for the problem. An example of this was the crisis that hit Source Perrier when traces of benzene were found in its bottled water. Instead of accepting responsibility, the company claimed that the contamination resulted from an isolated incident. It then recalled only a limited number of Perrier bottles in North America.

When benzene was found in its bottled water in Europe, an embarrassed Source Perrier had to announce a worldwide recall on the bottled water. Apparently, consumers around the world had been drinking contaminated water for months. The company was harshly attacked by the media for having little integrity and for disregarding public safety.

Johnson & Johnson, on the other hand, was praised by the media for its socially responsible actions. Along with the nationwide alert and the Tylenol recall, it established relations with the Chicago Police, the FBI and the Food and Drug Administration so that it could play a part in searching for the person who laced the Tylenol capsules and help prevent further tampering.

An article by Jerry Knight, published in *The Washington Post* on 11 October 1982, applauded the company for being honest with the public. 'Johnson & Johnson has effectively demonstrated how a major business ought to handle a disaster. ... This is no Three Mile Island accident in which the company's response did more damage than the original incident.' It observed that the company never attempted to do anything other than try to get to the bottom of the deaths. 'What Johnson & Johnson executives have done is communicate the message that the company is candid, contrite, and compassionate, committed to solving the murders and protecting the public.'

Johnson & Johnson also offered to exchange all Tylenol capsules that had already been purchased for Tylenol tablets. It was estimated that millions of bottles of Tylenol capsules were in consumers' homes at the time. Although this proposition cost the company millions more dollars, and there may not have been a single drop of cyanide in any of the capsules that were exchanged, the company made this choice on its own initiative in order to preserve its reputation.

Tylenol, which had a massive advertising budget prior to the poisonings, had become the number one alternative to Aspirin in the nation. The product had 37 per cent of the market for over-the-counter painkillers. Because it was such a huge money-maker for Johnson & Johnson, the company unleashed an extensive marketing and promotional programme to bring Tylenol back to its position as the number one analgesic in the USA.

Chairman of the board, James E. Burke said, in regard to the comeback, 'It will take time, it will take money, and it will be very difficult; but we consider it a moral imperative, as well as good business, to restore Tylenol to its pre-eminent position'.

In November, less than six weeks after the nation learned of the sudden deaths in Chicago, Johnson & Johnson subsidiary, McNeil Consumer Products, revealed its public relations plan for the recovery of Tylenol, at its sales conference in New Jersey. There were five main components of the McNeil/Johnson & Johnson comeback crusade:

- Tylenol capsules were reintroduced in November with a new triple-seal tamper-resistant container. This was appearing on market shelves by December, making McNeil the first company in the pharmaceutical industry to react to the Food and Drug Administration's new regulations and the national mandate for tamper-resistant packaging.
- To persuade customers who had been scared off the brand to return to using Tylenol, McNeil provided $2.50-off coupons that were good towards the purchase of any Tylenol product.
- Sales people at McNeil planned to recover former stock and shelf facing levels for Tylenol by putting a new pricing programme into effect. This gave consumers discounts as high as 25 per cent.
- A totally new advertising campaign was put in the works. The programme was launched in 1983.
- Finally, over 2250 salespeople were asked by Johnson & Johnson to make presentations to people in the medical community. These presentations were made by the millions to promote support for the reintroduction of Tylenol.

The comeback was a great success that turned a potential disaster for the company into a reason for their consumers to trust them even more than they had before the crisis.

How Orange became a trusted brand

Jeremy Dale, Vice President, Brand Marketing, Orange

Customer loyalty has been the key to the success of Orange. Increasingly, in today's corporate world, businesses are focusing more of their attention on building customer loyalty. Loyalty comes as a result of building a strong customer relationship, and the starting point for any lasting relationship is trust.

Trust, as always, has to be earned. The level of trust a customer has in an organisation does not remain constant: it can grow or it can wane. In the future, the most successful companies will be the ones that build customers trust and, as a result, enjoy customer loyalty.

The Orange brand was built on trust; trust gained by simply doing the right thing for the customer. Per-second billing, no ouch in our voucher, 24-hour handset replacement were just a few of the visible demonstrations that were evidence of Orange being committed to doing the right thing for its customers. In a market that had been long associated with bogus promises and hidden charges, customers embraced a company that they could trust. Retailers would say that there were two types of people: some came in and asked 'to buy a mobile phone' and others would say they want 'to join Orange'. Orange became like a movement.

If visibly doing the right thing for the customer is vital in establishing a basis for trust, then consistently delivering on the basics is essential in protecting that positive foundation. Customers need to trust that a company is not only 'batting' for them but also will deliver for them. Customers are gained one at a time and they are lost one at a time, and every interaction is important. Companies need to be ruthless in eradicating errors because every bad experience chips away at the trust the customer has and conversely every good experience strengthens the bonds of trust.

There are always defining moments in any relationship, and there is no more significant moment of truth than when something goes wrong. While this is a threat to the trust that already exists, it is also the biggest opportunity that a company has to build further trust. If problems are corrected swiftly and the customers are treated with empathy, then they feel that the faith they placed in the company is justified. Indeed, when trust is confirmed, trust is enhanced.

My experience is that the way in which a company handles a problem has far bigger consequences than the original problem itself. If it is handled well then the positive impression far outweighs the negative effect of the original problem. But if it is handled badly, that is usually a much bigger cause of dissatisfaction for the customer than the original problem was.

There is no excuse for treating customers badly. I once heard a wonderful story of a company that had a zero tolerance approach to the attitude that their staff had to their customers. It was a large life insurance company; it had several million customers and had 72,000 customer complaints in one year. This fell to 312 the following year and a little over 100 the year after. It achieved this by introducing just one rule. The company took the view that, given that a high number of calls were from people who had just lost a loved one, there was no excuse for them to ever be treated without care and empathy. They introduced a rule that if ever there was a complaint about a member of staff that person's boss had to go and visit the customer in person the following morning, apologise and resolve the problem. It didn't take many trips to Middlesborough on a Saturday morning for the managers to accept responsibility for their people's behaviour.

This one rule had a tremendous impact on many levels. It demonstrated internally the company's expectations about how customers should be treated. It penalised bad performance as determined by the ultimate judge – the customer – and it ensured that managers accepted the responsibility that their teams had to protect the company's most valuable asset: the trust of their customers.

Any company seeking to build trust with its customers must recognise that trust only comes with interactions, and the most customer-focused companies do two things: they strive to increase the number of interactions and they also maximise the impact of every one of them.

At Orange we positively encourage our customers to regularly visit our high street stores where our people (who are now called Phone Trainers rather than Sales Executives) show people how their phones can be more useful to them (they demonstrate, they don't sell). This initiative has had outstanding results, with customers regularly bringing back sandwiches or chocolates for our phone trainers as a way of saying thank you.

I have detailed above four principles that I believe are vitally important in building customer trust. They are:

- Demonstrate that you do the right thing for your customers.
- Be ruthless in eradicating errors and getting the basics right.
- Seize the defining moments in customer relationships to build trust.
- Strive for more interactions with your customers and make each one count.

To succeed in these four areas will undoubtedly bring increased loyalty and customer trust. Delivering all of these requires investment in your front line people. But more than anything else, the leaders of the organisation need to demonstrate an obsession with protecting and building the company's most valuable asset: the trust of its customers.

The basics of building customer trust

With this in mind, what actions can you take to develop and amplify the trust of your customers?

There is a simple process that helps to build trust (Figure 7.1). Missing one stage takes you back to the start, and makes it harder to build trust in the future. This approach can be taken with team members or clients – wherever trust needs to be built.

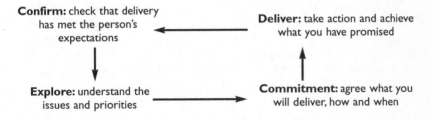

Confirm: check that delivery has met the person's expectations

Deliver: take action and achieve what you have promised

Explore: understand the issues and priorities

Commitment: agree what you will deliver, how and when

Figure 7.1 The trust-building process

Trust busting or trust building: the tricky business of hiring consultants

Most organisations hire consultants these days. Their ability to build trust is not normally one of the criteria in the decision to hire, at least not explicitly. Trust however is paramount, especially in coaching, where the relationship is characterised by the need for openness, and therefore confidentiality. Here is a view from a coach on how to develop client trust.

Developing client trust: a fresh perspective

Karen L. Otazo, Ph.D.

'Relationships of trust depend on our willingness to look not only to our own interests, but also the interests of others' (Peter Farquharson, early twentieth-century English cricketer).

You have just hired a consultant who is asking lots of questions, gathering intelligence about your organisation. But will this information merely help develop the consultant's skills? Or will it actually benefit your organisation?

Bringing consultants into your organisation can be a great way to develop strategy or innovative ideas, get new perspectives and buy expert knowledge or even an 'extra pair of hands'. However, hiring a consultant is a tricky business: the nature of the consulting relationship determines whether the company gets what it needs, or just throws money down a consulting black hole.

Although a company 'borrows' talent from a consultant, rather than 'buying' an employee, the process still involves a major commitment in terms of both time and money. For the consultant, in turn, the assignment can affect his or her financial situation and professional reputation.

Here are some 'trust builders' and some 'trust busters' which companies and consultants need to heed.

Trust busting: the 'taxi driver' approach

'You don't think like a consultant' is one of the best compliments I have ever received. It made me realise that I see myself as partnering my clients, as part of their organisation. I therefore find it strange when clients want to hire me by the hour, or even by the minute!

I was once dealing with a prospective client from a supply chain back-ground, who spent the whole time penny-pinching every aspect of the contract. That client was so used to taking farthings off widgets that he focused on the wrong aspects. He just didn't 'get it' when I tried to focus

---

on the outcomes – what I was there to assist with after all - rather than the specifics of the process. Such a 'taxi driver' approach didn't engender enough trust for me to continue. I pulled out of the process.

With few exceptions, I no longer work like a 'taxi driver'. I have found that seeing consulting as day labour turns consultants into day labourers rather than partners in a project's success. And true partnership is essential for a trust relationship to develop.

A high-level client once said that as a workshop I gave had lasted only six hours, they should not have to pay for the entire eight-hour day. However, it had taken me days to prepare that workshop. It is also near impossible to squeeze two more hours into a workshop day! That penny-pinching experience amazed me. Such situations demonstrate why daily fees do not make sense for excellent consulting work.

Trust building: the relational contract

The way that a consultant or a firm approaches contracting is reveal-ing. Are they happy to spend as much time as the process takes? One of my contracts took nine months to complete. As a result, everyone involved had 'buy in'. The contracting included a negotiated 'package', or programme price with all expenses and expectations built in, includ-ing a roadmap for the client to follow as they worked with the consul-tant. This advance programme package price created a commitment for both sides, and a relational contract as opposed to a contractual relationship.

In the nine-month contracting period there were actually three consultants involved. When one let down his clients, I honoured my commitment to the company and worked with the disappointed executives.

My bottom line in consulting is that there must be *generosity of spirit* on the part of both consultant and company. This means giving more than the contract stipulates when necessary, and being responsive to the other's needs. For example, when one of my clients was going through a major transition, I decided to give him more time during a period of personal crisis. He worked for a company that has never questioned my work or billings, and that has supported my work internationally.

Being a consultant is like being a short-term employee. Just as employees 'hold' the needs of their job and their company in their con-sciousness, an excellent consultant will 'hold' clients and their needs in his or her thoughts and plans beyond the actual assignment. The process of 'holding' the needs of the client over time is both a joy and an integral part of the consulting work.

Trust busting: 'one-trick ponies' and 'consultant creep'

'The people I distrust most are those who want to improve our lives but have only one course of action.' (Frank Herbert, twentieth-century science fiction author)

Although I have done many things in my corporate and consulting life, my expertise is in the coaching and assessment of individuals and teams. I also have a long list of other experts whom I recommend to clients because of their expertise or geographical location. Nobody can be an expert at everything. In corporate life, I once hired a consultant who excelled at empowering personal assistants in their work with executives. When asked to resolve a conflict within a group of personal assistants, however, she overstepped her expertise and failed miserably. Such 'one-trick pony' situations are not uncommon, and care should be taken to prevent them.

In my consultant hiring days, I especially disliked it when consultants whom I had brought into the company undertook additional work without telling me. I would then receive invoices to pay for work I did not know they were doing! It is the consultant's responsibility to keep the company representative informed of every request for additional consulting. As a client, I wanted to keep track in order to avoid 'consultant creep': consultants running amok in the organisation. One particularly disturbing element of 'consultant creep' was the 'end run' that consultants did by going directly to the top executives, while bypassing the person in charge of executive development.! The only way I could ensure that I had the right person in place for the task was to vet each request, and the appropriateness of the consultant for it.

One memorable example of consultant creep was a strategy consultant from a major consulting firm who was used to the big ideas and concepts of his craft. When the executives he worked with needed personal help with their leadership of change, he started coaching programmes for them without checking with me. Unfortunately, his knowledge of interpersonal skills, leadership behaviour and motivation was nil. What made him think that he could do this kind of work? He saw working with people as an extension of strategy. After his clients complained that they were not being helped he explained that he had the right background for coaching on people skills since he was certified in the 'Seven Habits of Highly Effective People'. It became obvious that he saw people as movable bits of strategy and any resistance on their part a failure of theirs. I quickly brought in a consultant with the right people skills and knowledge of leadership.

Trust building: telling 'truth' to power

It is all too easy for consultants to be sycophants rather than to say what needs saying to powerful individuals. If they are to learn, executives must be told what they need to hear rather than what they want to hear. A good consultant takes responsibility for moving individuals, or the collective culture, to action. The 'push' needs to be strong enough to provoke action, but gentle enough not to cause reactive 'push back' or organisational resistance.

One executive who was unhappy with another consultant indicated that he wanted to work with me because I am 'tough.' According to him I tell the 'truth' so that clients have to pay attention. I was a bit chagrined, but I understood. I realized that I understand the role of consultant as a type of catalyst. We have enormous impact, engender positive change, yet play no part in the kudos and get no 'strokes' for our work.

A trusting consultant–client relationship is by no means an easy thing to build. Developing a partnership of trust takes time. By investing in the trust-building process, and keeping an eye out to avoid trust busters, everyone stands to gain. Working together, client and consultant can construct a mutually beneficial working relationship, where both parties get more than they expect and give more than is expected of them.

LESSONS ABOUT BUILDING CUSTOMER TRUST

Trust and customers are a heady combination. Clearly, sales decisions are tough and unforgiving, and one wrong move can easily hand the initiative to competitors. Moreover, individual customers' perceptions, once formed, can be difficult to alter. Decisions that build trust need to be informed by an understanding of customers, a commitment to service and a focus on profitability, yet applying these principles is often difficult. As we have seen in the cases we have explored in this chapter, there are several ways to gain and maintain the loyalty and trust of customers. Here are some of the basics:

- View the situation from the customer's perspective.
- Make your commitments and stick to them.
- Avoid basing decisions about customers on assumptions. Sustaining a productive dialogue with them is much more beneficial, giving greater insights of a higher quality.
- Share information and insights about customers throughout the organisation, as this helps to coordinate activities and decisions. After all, success is much more likely if decisions are based on the same information and perceptions. Also, discussions with colleagues and others

involved in key decisions (such as agents) can be invaluable in ensuring success.

- Highlight the product's benefits, not simply its features, and highlight where it *genuinely* compares favourably to those of competitors.
- Build the customer's loyalty to your business and respect for your brand. If there is something about your business that appeals to customers, then identify this and develop it. Customers will then be much easier to keep.
- Consider using a range of incentives to close the deal that customers actually value, such as discounts or easier payment terms.
- Compete by developing uniqueness: either unique insights into customer needs that competitors do not possess or innovative features in the product or sales process that are distinctive and popular – or both.
- Act quickly and decisively to impress or reassure customers. Hesitation, for whatever reason, may be interpreted as a lack of concern.
- Manage and update information systems so that they serve customers in all these ways, ensuring a supportive approach.

Above all: when you are making changes or something goes wrong – tell them what is going on ...

Open communication with customers is crucial to maintaining their trust. Involving them in your business is a valuable way to gain and develop their trust and understanding. This does not mean patronising or giving away sensitive information, but it might mean explaining in general terms what plans you have to develop the business for the future, and specifically how these will benefit customers. It may also involve introducing members of your organisation, helping customers to understand how you work and where they can go for information or help.

Generally, trust with customers is strengthened when they are kept informed, and this is particularly true in difficult times. Johnson & Johnson did this well during the Tylenol crisis. Customers value information, so for example it may be useful at certain times to ask what they most want to know; openly share available information; provide it before customers ask, and check their understanding to see whether they need further clarification.

Displaying honesty and openness is particularly significant for building trust with customers, and is one of the secrets of developing a brand that is recognised, valued and effective.

... and consider the implications of your actions

You should understand the full implications of any actions for each customer or group of customers. For example, who is affected, what is the likely result, and will the outcome set an undesirable precedent? What signal will it give to others? Remember to consider the longer-term picture: customers are typically at a distance (unlike employees, who are typically much more available and present), so changing their perceptions is difficult and potentially arduous and demanding, often requiring significant resources.

TRUST OR BUST

As the examples of these businesses have shown, there is no need for confusion when it comes to customers, companies, trust, brands and loyalty. What matters to the customer is what matters to anyone else: a practical, straightforward approach emphasising honesty, simplicity, fairness, efficiency, initiative, respect and excellence. The firms we describe have succeeded because they realise several vital truths about trust and customers:

- *Success is mutual.* Profiting at the expense of customers is doomed to fail; relationships based on trust are the only sure foundation for profitability, and 'win–win' solutions are essential.
- *Complexity can diminish trust.* Customers give their trust expecting speed, responsiveness and service, and these are jeopardised by complexity. If you want customers to continue trusting you, keep it simple.
- *Recognition builds trust.* Everyone responds better when their value is acknowledged, so whether the success is a customer's or someone serving a customer, recognising their achievements builds understanding, community spirit and trust.
- *Clear communication is vital.* Maintaining trust means listening, valuing two-way communication, being honest and learning from people's comments.
- *Be consistent.* 'Walking the talk' and practising what you preach is essential for anyone – and most of all for customers.

Maintaining the trust of customers is challenging at any time, but it is particularly exacting given the changing nature of customers' needs. In the next chapter, we consider a closely related issue: how to develop trust during times of change.

8   Trust in times of change

There is much literature about managing 'change', reflecting the fact that it has become a subject of major concern for companies. Indeed, a whole profession of 'change consultants' has emerged. So why is it that companies tend to mishandle change? Why do we still hear tales of people being told they are redundant by text message or email?

In this chapter we look at the challenge for organisations of handling change. We examine the central role that trust holds in managing change effectively.

THE CHALLENGE OF CHANGE

Change is a tough thing for most people to handle. For organisations, it is often when they are going through significant periods of change that the trust of their employees matters most. Trust provides a sound and solid basis for new initiatives and actions, especially when finding a new course involves tough decisions about people's livelihoods. You can be sure that in such circumstances relationships will be tested. If they are not built on trust, then the change will be unnecessarily difficult.

The change curve

The human reaction to change has been extensively studied. The change process is commonly understood by reference to the research on people's reaction to bereavement. Elisabeth Kubler-Ross has been a major contributor to our understanding of the experience of loss, bereavement and redundancy.[1] The stages of loss that people typically go through are now commonly known as 'the change curve', which organisations often refer to in the context of job loss and redundancy. Dr Kubler-Ross undertook her research on dying by interviewing terminally ill patients. Although this is one of the most extreme and disturbing changes that anyone can face, the reactions to it are the same as for many less traumatic kinds. Dr Kubler-Ross's work led her to identify five stages that people go through.

1. *Denial ('no, not me')*. This is a typical reaction when patients learn that they are terminally ill. Denial, says Dr Kubler-Ross, is important and necessary. It helps cushion the impact of the realisation that death is inevitable.
2. *Rage and anger ('why me?')*. The patient resents the fact that others will remain healthy and alive while he or she must die.
3. *Bargaining ('Yes, me, but ...')*. Patients accept the fact of death but strike bargains for more time.
4. *Depression ('Yes, me')*. First, the person mourns past losses, things not done, wrongs committed. Then he or she enters a stage of 'preparatory grief', getting ready for the arrival of death.
5. *Acceptance ('My time is very close and it's alright')*. Dr Kubler-Ross describes this stage as neither happy nor unhappy. It is devoid of feelings but it is not resignation; it is really a victory.

People who are made redundant can go through a similar process. We would add a preliminary stage to this process before denial: that of *shock* or disbelief. We have witnessed people in shock following news of their redundancy. It can take a long time for people to reach the acceptance stage and people often oscillate between the different stages. During my career, I (Jeremy) was made redundant, and my initial feeling was certainly one of shock and fear. I was very concerned about my family, as we relied on my salary to support my wife and children. I was also concerned about what it might mean for my career in the longer term. In fairly short order, my thoughts turned to the second and third stages, oscillating between denial, intense disappointment and resentment. While I accepted the fact of redundancy quite quickly, I tried to find the best approach to get through it and back on track, adopting a practical, pragmatic approach. The 'bargaining' phase, born of necessity, was useful nonetheless in helping me to look forward, make progress and avoid deep depression. My initial feelings of disappointment and worry (common, I am sure, to anyone who is suddenly made redundant) did not abate for some time. I was fortunate to have a supportive family around me highlighting the things in life that really matter. Acceptance was accompanied by understanding. I felt a strange mixture of continuing disappointment to be leaving – and in such circumstances – but also excited about the future and relieved to be away from people who would choose to make me redundant!

This process is well understood by professionals who specialise in managing people and managing change. However, there is rarely any evidence of that understanding being used to inform the way change is managed in organisations.

Managing change: the essentials

The first step in managing a change successfully is to have reliable information at your disposal. Even if the change is unwelcome, people at least feel confident that the company knows what they are doing and have some comfort in its professionalism and expertise. This is a basic level of trust: trusting the competence and capability of those in charge. You might say this is a hygiene factor.

The second essential is for people to truly believe that you have their interests at heart and that they can trust you to do the best you possibly can to take care of them during the change. Too many executives treat redundancy as a process. Furthermore, the aspects of the process are often led by legal requirements instead of any human considerations. Returning briefly to the story of my own redundancy: as it was taking place and the trigger was being pulled, I remember my manager avoiding eye contact and reading from a pre-prepared script. No doubt he was wary, unsure how I would react, but it seemed to me that his expressions of thanks, regret and attempts at being supportive were part of a formal, scripted approach. If he really meant these sentiments, then they were being undermined by an emphasis on process.

Of course, changes such as redundancy do not just affect those who lose their jobs. Those who stay behind are affected too; their trust and confidence can be damaged seriously and permanently. Again, we all know the theory, but how many of us really pay attention to the needs of these people, the ones who are still running our organisation, serving our customers and need to be motivated to find and exploit opportunities?

In a fascinating book on the subject of redundancy, David Noer looks at so-called 'survivor sickness'.[2] In his research, the theme of distrust and betrayal came out strongly. Here is what two survivors said to him:

> My attitude is affected by what's gone on in the company, and I'm not so positive when I go out there and work. I think 'That's not my problem', where before my attitude was a lot different. I don't care whether the company, and I say *the company,* can support that customer in the middle of the night. It shouldn't be my problem: it's their problem. Let them find somebody else. I'm not going to go out there. That's the attitude I had to take a couple of times because I don't care anymore.

> I've lost trust in the company. I've been with them for eleven years, and I have no idea whether or not to trust them anymore because of what you hear positive from them about the company. The next day you come to work and it's 180 people out. You can't believe what they say. I've lost trust.

This reaction and loss of trust is common. The impact on the business of reduced commitment, even sabotage, by the workforce is extremely difficult to measure but can clearly be huge.

The reality is that for organisations to maintain trust in a period of massive change, especially if it involves job loss, is very difficult. It is possible to achieve but it takes commitment, continuous attention and, above all, the intention to do it well.

Few do it well or succeed. Let us look at an example of a company that did.

SUCCEEDING SPECTACULARLY AND UNUSUALLY AT CHANGE

Here is an unusual story about organisational change. It is unusual because it is the story of a company that handled it extremely well – so well that it could hardly be faulted. It is the story of a subsidiary of BT, a company called BT Marine (BTM), which was bought by Cable and Wireless Marine (CWM). A large number of redundancies were inevitable. The CEOs of each company got together and discussed the situation. Although they knew that one of them would not survive the merger, they decided that they would make every effort to make sure that they did their best to manage this change very well. First, they spent a huge amount of time and effort personally talking to staff from both companies about their intentions. They did it together and they talked to each other's staff. It came across that they were both committed to the people as well as the commercial outcomes. They stated that this was an integration of two companies, not a takeover. They were adamant that these were two excellent companies already and that they wanted to make sure that bringing the two together resulted in an even better organisation and future. They hired a consultancy firm to help (not necessarily a promising sign in many organisational change situations) and emphasised that this was an important process that they were committed to doing as well as they possibly could. They created an integration team of people from both organisations. I was on this team and admit I was sceptical and guarded at first. It was a tough time, as we all knew that half of us would lose our jobs. However, we believed what the bosses were saying. We really did believe that this was a transparent process. After a while everyone realised that they were not hiding anything and that they truly intended to integrate the company fairly. They said they would give the best people the jobs and that the people who were made redundant would be treated fairly. The external consultants helped and supported the process, and were valued for their objectivity and diligence. We all soon realised that they were true to their word.

> For organisations to maintain trust in a period of massive change is very difficult. It requires commitment, continuous effort and, above all, the intention to do it well.

The integration team comprised people representing all parts of the businesses and functional areas, ensuring that all perspectives could be covered. The team worked on a detailed project plan and implemented it with the help of the consultants. Communication was regular, efficient and honest. There were various mechanisms to ask questions and share the answers. A huge amount of effort and time went into keeping people informed, and even when there was no additional news, then people would be told that. We all felt as though nothing was being hidden. Another key part of the implementation was intensive training for all managers, helping them to support people who would be leaving the company and those who would be staying. This training focused on equipping managers with the knowledge, skills and confidence to be able to deal with many situations. It included helping people to think through their options, knowing when to refer the person to specialist support, handling a meeting where they told someone they did not have a job, communicating with that person's colleagues and being able to manage their own stress levels. It was time-consuming, expensive and extremely valuable. Managers felt supported and much more confident, and the employees saw that they really mattered. A few mistakes were made along the way, but with the reservoir of goodwill and understanding, people were more forgiving because they knew the company was genuinely trying its best to handle the situation humanely and efficiently. A positive but unintended consequence of the way this change was managed was that people from the two companies bonded and started to see each other as colleagues in the same boat. This quickly dissipated any feelings of animosity, which was a refreshing change from the usual feelings in such a situation. Many companies that merge live with an 'us and them' legacy for long afterwards, but BTM and CWM did an excellent job of removing that before the integration was complete.

While there were hitches along the way and the process was not perfect, I know of no one who was made redundant from that company who had a bad word to say about how they or their colleagues had been treated. I cannot think of any other company that that is true of. It was a master class in how to effectively manage a difficult change.

What can be learned about trust from this example? The first and most striking lesson was the work of the two CEOs to develop a trusting relationship with each other. This trust showed that they created a united front and clearly worked together for the greater good. At first, people did not believe this, but gradually, as they practised what they preached and were seen to act consistently, people realised it was true. The other important step these two CEOs took was admitting that they did not know how to make this work well and were not afraid to bring in outside support. They displayed total commitment to the process and to doing an excellent job. Also, they worked hard at considering every detail. The 'people' aspect of the change was clearly a central and important part of it – not just an optional extra, as it is in many companies. The CEOs displayed a real desire to get it right as well as a genuine understanding of people and how they cope with change. As a process, it acknowledged that the emotional part of coping with change is as important as the logical explanations. Neither of them hid behind the consultants (as many organisations do), but admitted that they needed help from consultants and then worked with them to make everything go as well as possible. Last, but by no means least, they communicated effectively, sustaining the confidence and trust of the staff, who felt well informed.

These two CEOs demonstrated that they cared, through their actions as well as their words. They quickly built trust in themselves and the process. The result: a company that was better than the two parts; a workforce that was committed and motivated, and the understanding of those people who ended up leaving.

DOES IT HAVE TO COME FROM THE TOP?

Received wisdom about managing during times of change is that change can only happen successfully when it is led from the top. Our experience is that this is not so. It is possible to create it from the middle outwards. Here is an example of some people who did that in an organisation called Epiphany.

Epiphany, in common with many organisations, was managed in 'silos' – vertical business divisions. Each business had a strong-minded, independent business head. The managers all had successful businesses and focused very much on the growth of their own particular unit. Although they had many customers in common, they sold different products and services and did not collaborate much. Then things started to challenge that way of working. Some customers wanted a single point of contact and asked for bundles of products and services to be put together from Epiphany. These requests caused a problem, as they meant that the sales people had to start sharing information and working together. They had never done that before. In fact, few of them knew any of their counterparts in other businesses. Their natural reaction was to go to their bosses for help and guidance. Amazingly, they didn't get it! Their bosses' targets and bonuses were all based on the results of their own business units. What is more, there was no appetite from the top to change any of the company's structures and systems so as to align the internal way of working with the customers' needs.

A couple of smart young sales people talked together about this situation. They were passionate about doing a fantastic job for the customers and it was anathema to them not to be able to do whatever was needed to satisfy their requests. They decided to seek out colleagues who felt the same. They collected a group of 'subversives' and started to talk about what they could do and how they could do it. Over a period of six months, they made it their business to start developing relationships with like-minded sales people in all of the other businesses. They were creating a network with a common purpose and a passion for what they believed in. The energy was tremendous. The success of their endeavours relied on trusting one another. What else was there to rely on? Most of their managers would have tried to put a stop to their activities if they knew. So these people had to find ways of doing their job while contacting and working with others on joint customer proposals, all 'under the radar screen'. They had to trust each other and they built that trust in a very short time. They were able to do that because they were very clear about why they were doing it: because it was what the customer wanted.

In less than a year, the subversives had achieved greater collective revenues, received excellent feedback from customers and established a strong trust network cutting across their business silos. Eventually they decided to go and tell the CEO of what they had done. He was amazed and impressed, giving them a budget for training, team meetings and a new bonus scheme.

Without trust, change damages businesses

This amazingly fast, powerful and effective organisational transformation succeeded because of the vision, intention and relationships of a few core people. If the CEO had hired a consultancy firm to deliver a programme of changes, they would probably still have been planning and 'selling it' in the time it took this group to make it happen. It is doubtful whether a formal change programme would have worked in any event, because the business heads did not see it as in their interest to work with each other.

Without doubt, it is relationships that make business happen and that make organisations function well or badly. If people have trusted relationships they can get on and do the right thing with absolute confidence that they have people around them who will help, support and challenge them instead of getting in the way, criticising and making their life difficult.

> It is relationships – with trust at their core – that make business happen and enable organisations to succeed. When people have trusted relationships, the result is greater clarity, focus and confidence about their course of action.

Without trust, change will never prosper or succeed. If people do not trust the company or do not believe the reasons that the company gives them for a particular course of action, they will expend at least some of their energy on unproductive activities. They will be looking for the hidden agenda, withholding information in order to increase their own sense of power. They will be wasting time, spreading discontent and complaining to colleagues about how they are being treated; their commitment and motivation will diminish.

So again, we see that trust is *the* basic ingredient for organisational success, whatever the context.

BETRAYAL AND CHANGE

When people feel betrayed, when there has been a massive breakdown of trust, it has to be re-established for any kind of change to succeed. This is as true in organisations where people have lost their jobs as for the high profile examples of betrayals of people by their governments.

Let us consider for a moment the word *betrayal*. It is a powerful, emotional and appropriate word for what can happen in organisations, and senior executives would do well to remember that. When people lose their jobs, they often feel a huge sense of betrayal. These feelings are often manifest in coping mechanisms such as blaming others and shifting responsibility, as well as a seemingly insatiable need for information. If there is no mechanism for acknowledging people's feelings and helping them to move on, then it is very difficult (if not impossible) for them to regain their trust.

In order to re-establish trust, betrayal needs to be acknowledged and people's feelings must be allowed expression, as is shown by the South African example. The South African government realised that when the trust of the people had been betrayed on such a massive, long-lasting and painful scale, as it had under the apartheid regime, people had to be given the opportunity to have that betrayal witnessed and acknowledged before being able to move on and regain trust. To do this, the government established the truth and reconciliation commission, which gave a major impetus to the task of healing national wounds.

A Fresh Perspective

Barbara Heinzen

Over the past five years, I have been working with groups of people in Kenya, Tanzania and Uganda, developing long-term scenario stories about the future of each country. I was hired by the Society for International Development in Rome, who wanted to use these stories to encourage broad public debate. At the first of five workshops in each country, I asked everyone in the room to introduce themselves by stating their 'pet passion', in order to uncover individual biases and preoccupations. In Kenya, where this work began, I used my own pet passion, the environment, as an example. However, this particular bias made it hard for some members of the Kenyan team to trust me. Since early colonial times, European policies have expropriated land for European uses. British settlers were the first to gain, but these government actions later included throwing people off the land to create national parks for wildlife. Given this history, my passion for the 'environment' reinforced a suspicion that Westerners cared more about East African wildlife than East African peoples, raising the ghost of earlier dispossessions.

About two years later, the work in Tanzania began. Once again, I asked people for their pet passions and once again I declared my own interests as an example. This time, however, I tried to articulate something about the working ecological knowledge of rural people in Africa and its potential value in an age of ecological distress. My pet passion, I said, was to imagine how an ecological model might come from Africa. This revision had the advantage of not generating instant suspicion, but it was incomprehensible. Many people in the room were young and had been educated abroad or grown up in the city of Dar es Salaam and had little experience of working life in the rural areas. More critically, their preoccupations were focused on an immediately pressing frontier: the need to overcome deeply engrained habits, including financial and intellectual dependency on international donors. Until this changed, it would not be possible to identify an alternative, African concept of ecological modernisation.

About a year later, a colleague and I began working in Uganda. As before, I asked people at the first workshop to state their pet passions and used my own passion about the invention of ecological societies as an illustration. By this time, I was convinced that African societies knew something about living ecologically that we in the North had forgotten. I therefore described my pet passion as 'what the North could learn from Africa, not just what Africa could learn from the North'. Once again, my enthusiasm fell on stony ground. In Uganda, the central distracting concern was political mistrust among Ugandans. Before our first workshop, we were told it might be difficult for people to talk honestly with each other after experiencing the political violence of Idi Amin and civil war. When we asked their passions, one participant said it was 'To have a Uganda which is very tolerant'. In this context, the defining issue of the country was not the threat of ecological damage, but of renewed violence.

What do these three stories tell us about trust and the capacity for social invention in post-colonial societies? All three encounters have several things in common, among them the perception that environment is a Western issue, not an African one. Around this perception are a number of unstated fears. First, there is a fear that the Western desire to maintain the biological abundance of African wildlife is actually a covert way of ensuring African peoples never industrialise and never compete directly with Western economies. Second, there is the very real experience – in all three countries – of seeing people thrown out of their homes to create national parks for animals. Environment, therefore, carries with it a genuine threat of dispossession in the name of Western ideals about an impossibly pristine wilderness. Third, for millennia, in various parts of the world, rural people have been seen as less 'civilised' than urban people. The suggestion that Africans might invent a non-industrial ecological future implies that Africans will remain in rural areas and, therefore, 'less civilised' and less worthy of respect. All these fears reinforce the conclusion that Western talk about the 'environment' is just a new conquest of Africans by other means.

There is another dimension to these three stories, however: the cultural experience of my East African colleagues. Since the nineteenth century, African societies have been viewed by European societies as 'primitive' cultures, soon to be replaced by modern ways. African philosophies, ethics, economic organisation, agronomy and political rules have been systematically denigrated and dismantled, destroyed as useless and backward institutions. That is why, when people talk about education in Africa, they usually mean education in a European language with a European curriculum. They rarely refer to oral knowledge passed on through stories, apprenticeship or practical experience. While such knowledge may survive in daily life, it is not respected as 'education' in the modern world.

In this context, African professionals who have struggled to acquire a European education were bound to mistrust a Westerner who suggested that the oral knowledge of their families and societies has value in the twenty-first century. Why has the story suddenly changed? What trick is behind this point of view? When the Kenyans heard me describe the environment as my pet passion, they must have wondered what I was trying to gain. Besides, many of them were successfully competing on Western terms. Why should they resurrect the rural African knowledge they had left behind? The Tanzanians' indifference to my pet passion may have had a different origin, rooted in their ambivalent dislike of donor dependence. Would my idea of an African ecological model reinforce long-standing patterns of dependence? Was I just another foreigner hoping to use Tanzania to test my own ideals? Finally, in Uganda, I was working with people who had experienced civil war and betrayal in their own lives. How could they have confidence in their own society when it had bred the disasters they had all seen? Why should they trust me to have more confidence in Ugandans than they had themselves?

So, one by one, I found that the people who have become my closest colleagues in East Africa had no place for my vision of an ecological future. This was personally disappointing, but irrelevant to my task as facilitator. Here I was more successful, as each country team developed a very different set of stories about the future of their society. These differences reassured me that I had largely kept myself and my views out of the conversation. Instead, the East African teams had done their own thinking, based on their own understanding of the world and how it works.

A trusted facilitator can propose new ideas, and if they resonate with people they will be adopted. As I watched my East African colleagues ignore my own convictions about the value of African ecological understanding, I asked myself why my thinking was so consistently rejected. Was I wrong? Was there nothing of value in African knowledge? Or was I right, but the established dreams of development were so convincing that any ecological alternative was just a romantic fairy tale? Had we simply failed to find a language for these ideas that we could all understand? Or was I simply not trusted? Was I too implicated – by birth and upbringing – in the injuries of colonialism and dependent development for anything I said to be heard without the filters of the past?

All these issues are relevant, but as I prepared for the last workshop in Uganda, I thought more about the question of self-confidence. How could the Ugandans trust who they were, given what they had been through? There is another reason why it was so hard for the idea of an ecological future in Africa to resonate with my colleagues. While prowling through the leading bookstores of Kampala with a friend, Abdu Simba, I noticed there was no environmental section. There were no textbooks describing important ecological principles, no academic studies about the environmental knowledge of rural people. There were only coffee table books with large illustrations of wild animals and happy natives, books that reinforced all the prejudices of the colonial past. 'No wonder no one understands me!' I said to Abdu, 'there is nothing on the environment here.' 'You might as well be speaking Chinese,' he replied.

This brief conversation raises a final issue about trust and social invention. Our understanding of ecology is relatively new. Our ability to integrate this understanding in our plans, predictions and assumptions is weak – not just in East Africa, but in every organisation I know. As often as not, ecological thinking is rejected simply because it is too new. When that happens, personal trust becomes critical. With such trust, individuals can experiment with the things that their own backgrounds have not equipped them to understand. Without it, we risk learning nothing new.

117

9   Building a culture of trust

As the Wall Street manager said to a young, terrified trader who had just lost a fortune on the trading room floor: 'Fire you? I just invested ten million dollars in your future with this firm.'

Some important truths about trust are that to establish it we need to invest in the learning not in blaming, we need to attend to the relationships not just the outcomes and we need to try and understand before we judge. In this chapter, we look at what it takes to build a culture of trust, what to do when trust is broken, the importance of rebuilding it and how that can be done.

A LONG TIME TO BUILD, AN INSTANT TO LOSE

Here is a story about a church organisation in the UK (though it could have come from any kind of organisation). It is the story of how a new leader set about building trust and how something that happened resulted in it being destroyed quickly. What is possibly different about this story is the effort that was put in to understand how it happened and what could be done to rebuild it.

John had been rector of his parish for seven years. During that time, he worked with the parishioners to develop a vision, strategy and goals. They did this through an open consultation process involving meetings that any of the 200-strong congregation were welcome to attend.

A couple of years ago things started to go wrong. The issue that eventually caused the rift was the church hall, which was inadequate and run down. John proposed that they set up a project to build a new one, and when the plan ran into opposition he tried to resolve the issue through a consultation process. One person in particular opposed the plan and led a group of others in a quest to stop it happening. John told me, 'I was staggered at how easy it was for all the positives, our common purpose and the trust we had built to break down'. It had been a dreadful experience for all concerned. He said that building the community had been a complex task involving bringing together many strands, aligning personal and community goals and developing a network of positive relationships. He told me that his consultative approach and the open meetings that he held had enabled him to gain people's trust. He was amazed that it had taken five years to build a trusting congregation and a matter of weeks to destroy it.

The breaking point came at one of the open meetings where Edward, the man leading the group who opposed the plans, gave a speech asking people to 'vote for John or me'. John did not support the idea of asking people to vote. He felt it was divisive. But it went ahead and 53 per cent of the people supported John. The effect has been that people are now very wary of him and feel that whatever he does he is doing it to try and get them over to his side. Edward has continued to level all sorts of accusations at John, in an overt attempt to undermine him and try and win supporters.

In a subsequent council meeting, four of the members called for Edward to resign because they felt that, having 'lost the vote', he should be supporting the majority. Edward refused. John told me that he would not have supported his resignation anyway, as he did not feel that was a positive way forward. He felt it would have widened the parish split and would have further served to damage trust. We talked about parallel situations when politicians resign and how that does not necessarily change anything; it just serves to find a 'scapegoat'.

John said that he is now trying to find a way of re-building the trust and healing the rift so that it does not damage the community on an ongoing basis. He wants to find a way of allowing people to speak about what went wrong and forgiving one another: a kind of communal absolution. He feels it is important not just to learn from the mistakes but to incorporate the lessons into the way things are done in the future. To do that he plans to do two things. He is going to commission someone to write a history of the parish so that this story, among others, is told and integrated into history in a positive way. Otherwise, he is afraid that it will always be remembered as a wholly negative time and continue to be a blight on the ability to rebuild trust in the community. He talked of how communities inherit history, including 'baggage'. 'If we don't heal it now, the legacy will continue.'

The other route that has been suggested to him is to employ a neutral third party who can listen and talk to John, Edward and any other members of the congregation. The mediator will then write a 'report' about what has happened and present it at some kind of event. The way John described it, I wondered whether it would be a kind of truth and reconciliation committee of the type that provided so much healing for the people of South Africa. The event would conclude with some symbolic act like the opposing parties meeting and shaking hands.

John told me that as a leader he is aware that the parishoners are feeling battered and bruised by the whole situation. He feels that the way forward is to give people the opportunity to express how they are feeling. He himself will do that. He feels that it is important in this process that he allows himself to be vulnerable to and expresses his own hurt, and talks of the things that he got wrong.

He is hopeful that they will be able to rebuild the trust but, as he said, it will certainly take longer to rebuild it than to create it in the first place. An important part of doing that is for everyone to show compassion for themselves and others and not continue to burden themselves with guilt for what happened.

WHAT IS A CULTURE OF TRUST?

High-trust organisations understand the key processes that need to be in place to build trust. The companies that are most successful at mergers and acquisitions appreciate that the process of trust creation is critical to success. It is an *either/or*. Either trust is created or it is not. There is no halfway house.

There are several characteristics that we have identified that are present in a culture of trust. These characteristics interact with each other to create an environment where, for the most part, people trust and are trusted. I say for the most part because it appears impossible to have *total* trust *all* the time.

- *Shared values.* These are values that are not just adopted at work but are important to people in their day-to-day lives. They do not necessarily have to relate to work but could be to do with the wider community and environment.
- *A shared mission or goal.* This is important: people need to be pulling in the same direction and to have a commitment to goals beyond just their own.
- *Open and authentic leadership.* Quite simply, the leader sets the tone. People pick up on the leader's values and motivations, whether or not they are explicitly stated. It is not possible to create a culture of trust if the leader is not trusted and does not trust others.
- *A culture of consensus not force.* To coerce people implies that unless you exert that pressure they will not fulfil a commitment or do the right thing. Trusting cultures are ones where people do things willingly.
- *A feeling of enjoying work.* If people feel relaxed and are not fearful of making a mistake, they are more likely to trust themselves and others.
- *An atmosphere of fun and enjoyment.* Innovation companies have shown that the most productive environments for innovating are ones where people can have fun; they are less afraid of making fools of themselves and so will try out ideas and concepts. Seeing people having fun in the workplace is a sign that the culture is one of trust and openness.
- *A desire to learn, not blame.* Again, this is linked to fear. In a culture of blame people cannot trust others and be open. If people detect even a hint that someone will be blamed for something going wrong, trust is destroyed.
- *Honesty and authentic conversations.* This is a basic requirement for trust. Without this there will always be misunderstandings and a holding back of information.

121

Looking at these characteristics, particularly the ones relating to shared values, it would be tempting to conclude that it is only the public sector or charitable organisations that can have any hope of creating a culture of trust. That is not so. We have examples of high-trust companies in the most unlikely place, the cleaning services industry: the Scandinavian company, SOL and the Chicago based company, Servicemaster. One would not expect employees in these companies to have a desire to be altruistic and do work that is of higher value to society. Yet they do share common values relating to customers and pride in their work.

The core distinguishing factor is a leader for whom a culture of trust is important. There are many who *say* that it is but do not follow through relentlessly to do what it takes to create trust. For these leaders, the nature of the culture is of secondary importance, despite their words; what really matters to them is hitting their targets.

In our example above, it mattered to John that he had built a culture of trust and that he now finds a way of genuinely rebuilding it, not just for the current members of the organisation but also for future generations. His desire to learn about the mistakes that he and others made and to find a way of moving on means that he at least stands a chance of succeeding. Without that, no improvement would be possible because there would be no honesty or authentic discussion.

An example of a much bigger organisation whose leader has built a high-trust culture is the Worldwide Wildlife Fund (WWF). Like John, the people who work for WWF care about the future and the legacy they will leave. The fund was officially founded on 11 September 1961 amid fears that habitat destruction and hunting would soon bring about the extinction of much of Africa's wildlife. It has grown from modest beginnings into a global conservation organisation that has been instrumental in making the environment a matter of world concern. It is an excellent example of a high-trust culture.

There are a number of factors that make this so. The Director General is described as having 'a very authentic voice'. People in the organisation around the world are willing to follow him because it is obvious from his background and his values that he really cares about conservation. The management team of WWF has a shared mission and common values. They are seen as trustworthy people who keep their word and are the first to admit when they are wrong. They are non-controlling. Their style is relaxed and informal. There is a strong culture of relationships, networks, coaching and communication.

The structure of the organisation also supports the culture of trust. WWF is network based and has a very flat structure. There are 53 autonomous national organisations around the world and four associate ones. Central support is provided from an office in Switzerland that sees itself as the 'air traffic control' of the whole organisation, not as a dictating central force. There is a committee that agrees on the main priorities, targets and milestones. It works by consensus and the offices do not have to follow its guidance. The sole purpose of the committee is to achieve the ultimate goal of making a difference to the planet.

WWF's mission, itself, attracts people with high values. When they are recruiting new staff they always ask them what they know about WWF's goals and what attracts them to want to work there. The answers to these questions give information about commitment and values. Like all high-trust organisations in any sector they hire on values as well as skills and experience. Dorothy Bray, Director of Human Resources Development, believes that WWF attracts people who have a high value-base because the organisation offers meaning, and it is the shared values and meaning that contribute to the high-trust culture.

Dorothy believes that if you trust people they will prove themselves to be trustworthy, and says that WWF operates on that assumption. She related a story of the heat wave in Switzerland in the summer of 2003. The temperatures were so high in the office that it was very uncomfortable, so they told their staff they could be flexible about their hours. They trusted them to make up the time when the weather got cooler. They were 100 per cent convinced that no one would abuse that trust.

> To wait until someone proves that they are trustworthy does not work. If you start by assuming that they are, they will invariably prove you right. Trust is reinforced by trusting.

This is one of the key factors of creating a culture of trust, whether in a one-to-one relationship or in an entire organisation: it is that you have to start by trusting. To wait until someone proves they are trustworthy does not work. If you start by assuming that they are, they will invariably prove you right. Trust is reinforced by trusting. If we have faith in people, we not only tend to have that trust confirmed but generally see more and more reasons to prove we are right to trust them. What is more, being trusted is so psychologically gratifying that people seek to do more things that reinforce your belief in them. It is a virtuous circle. It works the same way with mistrust: the less we trust, the more we find reasons to reinforce that lack of trust. If organisations did nothing else but apply this simple formula, they would succeed in increasing their trust quotient.

SIGNS OF A LOW-TRUST CULTURE

It is not difficult to spot a low-trust culture. When you pull apart the elements that make the culture untrusting, there are some you can immediately recognise as ones that obviously get in the way, and some which may be less obvious and maybe even more insidious.

- *Scepticism about the leader.* A leader who is seen as acting more for personal gain than for the greater good of the organisation will never be able to create a trusting culture. Trusted leaders are never viewed with indifference, either. Ask the people who work for them and they can usually tell you a lot about their leaders and what is important to them. That is because the true leaders inform their staff thorough words and actions and are transparent about what is important to them and what they expect from others.

- *Cynicism.* Cynicism is an attitude of mistrust. Today's society is becoming more and more cynical. In business it is almost expected; indeed, its absence is often perceived as weakness or foolishness. Cynicism is a refusal to trust. It closes off possibilities. It is damaging to organisations because its underlying attitude is one of 'I don't believe this, it will never work'. An attitude of cynicism provides no platform for building trust. It drains people's energy, causes them to lose hope and even not to bother. It is different from scepticism, which is about not being gullible.

> Cynicism is a refusal to trust. It closes off possibilities. It is damaging to organisations because its underlying attitude is one of 'I don't believe this, it will never work'. An attitude of cynicism provides no platform for building trust.

- *Foolish trust.* In a world where there is growing distrust, there are also extreme examples of an irrational desire to trust blindly. At a micro level we see it in recruitment practices in organisations. People are hired on the basis of a few hours of interviews, a track record and, as is often the case in senior appointments, a hope that they will single-handedly be able to change or rescue situations that others have been unable to resolve. On a larger scale, foolish trust is present where consultancy firms are hired to do projects when they know little or nothing about the market or industry concerned. This is a further example of hoping that someone else knows better than us and can sort out the problem. At its root is either negligence or a lack of self-trust.

- *Fear.* Low-trust cultures are characterised by fear of the boss, fear of making a mistake because of the repercussions and fear of losing one's job. The sort of behaviour that you see in such cultures is caution and lack of risk-taking, along with passive acceptance and lack of challenge to authority.

- *'Clever' communication (or spin).* When this kind of communication occurs in organisations it is a sign that openness and transparency are lacking. When messages are 'managed' very carefully, people become suspicious of what is really going on.

These factors are related to each other and are mutually reinforcing. Trying to address one of them in isolation – as organisational change programmes often do by focusing on a particular 'intervention' – will not work, because trust is systemic in nature. Nor does it work to address the surface level. Many organisations have gone the route of writing mission statements. Quite simply, unless (to use the old cliché) 'hearts and minds' are captured, that will not work.

CAN BROKEN TRUST BE MENDED?

We started our research with the assumption that there were people out there who had successfully repaired lost trust in relationships and organisations. In reality, we found people who doubt whether it is ever possible to fully recover from a breach of trust.

Dorothy Bray, Director of Human Resources Development for WWF International told me:

> For those very rare exceptions where trust has been misplaced, I do not have an answer. I believe it's like breaking a beautiful, precious piece of crystal: you may be able to glue the pieces together into something you can use again, but you will always see the join and it will never be the same. It reminds me of a poem my parents taught us when we were children:
>
> > On such fine threads, we hang our faith in living –
> > Trust is a thread one little word can break,
> > Not to be mended by the mere forgiving,
> > Not to be knotted for a friendship's sake.

We found people in organisations who had found ways of coping with missing trust. We found no one who claimed to have fully recovered lost trust.

Mistrust fenced off

This story is fiction, but it is based on some real experience. It is about an IT company I will call Innova, which was founded by four people.

All four founders had previously been involved in other start-ups and were wary about venture capital, so they did all they could to fund Innova using their personal financial resources. Jake, one of the four, was outstandingly good at finding economical ways to develop the specialist software on which Innova's business depended. Without this skill, software development might have proved several times more costly, making it impossible to do without external finance.

Innova prospered and took a good share of the niche market at which its products were aimed. As the business matured, it became clear that Jake had some serious personality flaws. Most of the time he was a rational person, articulate and amusing, but under stress he behaved destructively. Almost at random, he would bully and insult those around him. He would accuse colleagues of all kinds of dirty tricks, sometimes indulging in the very same tricks himself.

When they started the company, the four founders had agreed that none of them could be forced out of the business by the others. In any case, Jake's skills, essential at the start, were still valuable. So the others decided they would just have to live with him. This was quite hard to do. By then, about thirty people were working in the company and their work was seriously disrupted whenever Jake was in one of his bad moods. Some staff resigned, some only continued because of the support they got from one or more of the other three founders. It looked as if the whole enterprise could fall apart.

To compensate for their being unable to trust Jake, the other three realised that they would have to work hard on building trust among themselves. On Saturday mornings, the three had informal meetings at which they could let off steam about Jake's behaviour. They extended this trust building to the more junior people. Gradually they discovered how to put up a firewall around Jake when he started to behave badly. It took a lot of effort and was far from an ideal situation, but the business survived. Eventually Innova grew to a size that was interesting to a large company. A takeover offer was made and accepted by the four shareholders, who got a handsome return for their investment of effort and money. Under its new owners, the business continued to prosper.

By hard work and dedication, Innova found that an area of mistrust could be fenced off, within its generally trusting community.

In most organisations there are people who care about building trust and those who do not.

BUILDING A HIGH-TRUST ORGANISATION

There is one easy way to create an organisation of trust: only hire people for whom honesty, openness and trust are non-negotiable. If you do this you will transform the relationships within the organisation, along with its efficiency, productivity, customer satisfaction, relationships with suppliers and ability to innovate. This will ultimately increase success, which for business organisations means profitability.

A lot of organisations spend a huge amount of money on hiring consultants to change their organisations in some way. The essential need, though, is to create a culture that enables the organisation to better achieve its goal, which for business ultimately means increasing profits. Most of the big consultancy organisations offer products and services relating to organisation change. Most projects fail to deliver enough change to make a difference for one simple reason. It is because the underlying blockage to all organisational problems is a lack of trust. Quite simply, if trust relationships do not exist, the organisation can never reach its potential.

In this excerpt from his book *The Human Equation*, Jeffrey Pfeffer explains why building trust is a fundamental part of creating organisational change.

Three principles appear common to most of the successful transformations to high performance work practices that I have observed:

1. Build trust.
2. Encourage change.
3. Measure the right things and align incentive systems with new practices.[1]

He goes on to say:

The first and most fundamental principle – and, I might add, the most often violated – is to build trust. The essence of high performance work arrangements is reliance on *all* organisational members for their ideas, intelligence and commitment to making the organisation successful. Such efforts will not be forthcoming in the absence of trust. One occasionally hears that incentives or surveillance and control (or some combination of the two) can substitute for trust by affecting the environment in such a way that people do the right thing. But this view is naïve, for incentives and controls work only for behaviours that can be specified in advance. Moreover, these techniques for producing behaviour are invariably more costly than those built on trust and respect.

So, the first question that leaders should ask about any proposed practice is whether it is likely to build and main-

> Strangely enough, high-trust organisations don't pursue trust as one of their objectives. It is the result of the values that their leaders have.

tain trusting relationships. If the answer is no, the practice shouldn't be instituted – period. One way to build trust is by sharing information, including business and strategic plans, with all employees. This isn't always done because one of the incentives senior managers seem to enjoy is knowing things that others don't – knowledge is power and holding secrets can be a source of status. Let me suggest that this is a very costly incentive, however. By keeping things secret, the organisation conveys that it really doesn't trust its members. Conversely, sharing business plans, strategies, and, of course, operating information conveys the idea that all members are partners in the task of improving performance and that all have an important role in these efforts.

127

The first barrier to overcome in endeavouring to build a high-trust organisation is having a genuine awareness of what the benefits are.

Strangely enough, high-trust organisations do not have trust as one of their objectives. It is just the effect of the values that the leaders have.

And finally ... never forget that trust is the key

So it appears that high-trust organisations do not actively set out to build trust: they say they never even talk about it. In this respect, they are the same as low-trust organisations! The difference is that it is important to the former: it is such an integral part of their values that they do not even notice it. Low-trust organisations do not hold the values that result in their practices and actions leading to trust. Trust appears to be such an invisible quality that when it is absent in organisations we know that things are not working as they could, but we rarely diagnose lack of trust as a cause. A study that illustrates this point nicely is Dale Zand's simulation of managerial problem solving and Boss's replication of his study several years later.[2] Both studies looked at how high-trust and low-trust conditions affected the quality of managerial problem solving. Each study gave a number of teams a task and a set of instructions; some of the instructions had low-trust assumptions, some had high-trust assumptions.

The instructions for the high-trust teams were as follows:

> You have learned from your experience during the past two years that you can trust the other members of the top management team. You and the other top managers openly express your differences and your feelings of encouragement or of disappointment. You and the others share all relevant information and freely explore ideas and feelings that may be in or out of your defined responsibility. The result has been a high level of give and take and mutual confidence in each other's support and ability.

The instructions given to the low-trust group were 'worded to induce a decrease in trust'.

In the high-trust teams, there was a high degree of reciprocity including expressing differences of opinion, encouraging others, expressing disappointment, sharing information and offering support. The opposite was implied of the low-trust teams.

Both the Zand and the Boss studies indicate that high trust was the key factor in problem-solving effectiveness. What is even more interesting is that, in his replicated studies, Boss reports the following:

> *The fact that trust was the overriding variable was not initially apparent to the subjects.* When participants were asked to explain the reasons for the obvious differences in team effectiveness, they offered a number of

plausible explanations. When told of the different instructions, the group members reacted with amazement and relief. *They were amazed that they had not perceived what seemed to them after the fact to be obvious.*[3]

This study gives us a few clues about creating a culture of trust. Apart from corroborating the fact that performance and job satisfaction are increased with trust, it also demonstrates that managers do not perceive its importance. In explaining why something did not work well, they talk about lack of communication, personality clashes, the behaviour of the boss and unclear expectations. In Zand's and Boss's studies they did not notice the trust differential. In real life we seem not to notice that either. *This is a big lesson for organisational leaders and consultants ,who may be ignoring the very thing that can create the culture change that they want.*

Different perspectives: building a culture of inter-disciplinary trust in education

Elaine M Cronk, M.Ed.

Of many successful days, I recall one in particular which serves to illustrate the culture of trust that we had developed in the school, and in particular among the different professions. I walked into one of the classrooms where a science lesson was being led by the dietician; the occupational therapist was assisting those children who required specific help to write their notes; the teacher was checking composition, grammar and the like; the physiotherapist was giving input relating to nutrition and exercise; and the psychologist was working with a child who had attention deficit disorder on strategies for concentration.

At the same time a nurse was making observations on another child and the classroom assistant was showing a child how to record work on the computer.

The following morning at our team meeting we discussed the results/observations of this session and formulated plans for goals to achieve.

This would not have been possible without the crucial element of trust. All these professionals were so secure in their own specialised field that input from other colleagues was regarded not as criticism or censure but as an efficient and productive method of problem solving to enhance each child's recovery.

The issue of trust may at first appear to be most relevant to each of us in our personal lives, and then within our working environment.

Within the private business sector, trust can be used to raise brand awareness or perhaps to increase productivity. In the public sector, where there were no targets or waiting times to be met, the value of trust as a

---

means to enhance productivity may not have seemed important in the past. The current trend of moving further away from government controls offers more opportunities and indeed there is an increasing need for trust to be addressed inside this sector.

During the mid-late 1990s I was privileged to be part of an innovative and unique school for children in hospital in the south of England. The success of this was largely a result of real trust between professions. It was the vision of a consultant paediatrician that a service, based within a large teaching hospital, could utilise the massive potential of a multidisciplinary service to support the recovery of children with non-acute but nonetheless debilitating, often serious and sometimes even life-threatening conditions.

Crucial to the success of the service was the need to assemble a team that would be able to look beyond their individual fields of expertise, without being protective or insular about their own knowledge in order to put the needs of the children first. Applicants for the posts were interviewed by an interdisciplinary team and this exercise helped to pave the way for the trusting partnership that ensued, and proved so successful.

In our professional lives it is a natural instinct to become protective and sometimes miserly of our own expertise. After all we have invested years of our lives training to high levels of competence and knowledge in our chosen field. Some may question how a colleague without that specialised training could possibly offer an opinion or assist with problem solving.

I was extremely fortunate and considered it a great privilege to be appointed to the team. My colleagues were also experts within their own professions and included

- the Consultant Paediatrician and Senior Registrar (who because the children were hospital patients were the lead professionals)
- myself
- a head teacher
- my team of teachers and classroom assistants
- a consultant child psychiatrist
- the ward manager (a senior nursing sister)
- her team of nursing and support staff
- a paediatric psychologist
- a senior paediatric physiotherapist
- a senior paediatric occupational therapist
- a senior paediatric dietician
- a senior social worker.

The vision became reality, made possible by each individual not just allowing access to his or her notes, thoughts and discussions but positively encouraging the dialogue.

10 Measuring trust

He who mistrusts most should be trusted least.

(Greek proverb)

We regularly make decisions about whether we can trust people. We usually do so based on 'gut reaction' and previous experience of individuals or evidence of whether they can be trusted. A decision to trust someone can be crucial. Getting it wrong can cost money, as in the case of hiring someone who turns out not to be trustworthy. It can also cause irretrievable damage to relationships with customers and others for whom a trusting association is crucial.

In this chapter, we explore the conundrum of measuring trust, and provide practical guidance for assessing levels of trust in yourself and others.

SWEATY PALMS AND NOSE-SCRATCHING

During our research for this book, we spoke to a psychologist and asked him whether trust could be measured. Unsurprisingly, the answer we got was that it was extremely difficult. However, he said that it was possible to establish indicators of trust based on people's answers to questions about values. There are also physiological measures. They involve wiring someone up, asking them questions and monitoring their heartbeat and perspiration levels as they respond to your questions. Wiring someone up and subjecting them to that kind of scrutiny could be enough to induce sweating and shaking in the most trustworthy of people. In so far as it is an effective measure, its value is in measuring whether the person lies in response to a particular question or set of questions, not whether he or she is a trustworthy person.

Jo-Ellan Dimitrius is a jury consultant in the USA. In her book *Reading People*,[1] she discusses the indicators of honesty and dishonesty:

> Honest people are generally relaxed and open. Dishonest people aren't. Any trait that shows tension, nervousness or secretiveness indicates possible

dishonesty. Lying is often easy to detect when you know what to look for. The symptoms listed here are reliable tip-offs to the occasional liar and frequent liar. These physical clues generally appear only when someone knows he's lying and is at least somewhat troubled when he does. Luckily, most people are at worst occasional liars and reveal their discomfort in many ways. Symptoms of dishonesty include:

- Shifty or wandering eyes.
- Any type of fidgeting.
- Rapid speech.
- Change in voice.
- Shifting back and forth on one's feet or in a chair.
- Any signs of nervousness.
- An exaggerated version of the 'sincere, furrowed-brow' look.
- Sweating.
- Shaking.
- Any activity that obscures the eyes, face, or mouth, such as putting the hand over the mouth while talking, rubbing the nose, or blinking the eyes.
- Licking lips.
- Running tongue over teeth.
- Leaning forward.
- Inappropriate familiarity such as backslapping, other touching, and getting too close (invading personal space).

The signs of honesty are just the opposite of those listed above. Honest people are relaxed, calm; they usually meet your gaze. A sincere smile and the warm, kind eyes that most of us know when we see them also indicate honesty.

When things get stressful, it can be difficult to tell the difference between honest nervousness or defensiveness and dishonesty. If your employee has made a horrible mistake and you've asked him to explain it, chances are he'll look nervous and defensive no matter how truthful he is. I've watched hundreds of nervous witnesses, and I've found the surest way to detect a lie in a stressful situation is to watch for their patterns of behaviour, looking for consistencies and deviations.

These tips may be useful to discover if a person is lying but they do not necessarily tell you whether that person is normally trustworthy.

We see things as we are, not as they are

Ultimately, we need to experience the person's commitment. We may decide that we will put our trust in a person, but we cannot know whether to trust them until they demonstrate their trustworthiness in some way. We may know their values to be good and their intention to be positive, but many things can get in the way of a person being deemed trustworthy.

Figure 10.1 illustrates what can go wrong and why people can fall at the 'beliefs' hurdle, showing themselves to be untrustworthy.

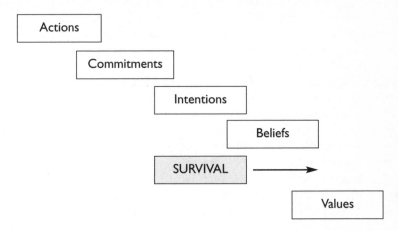

Figure 10.1 How trust can falter

People are born 'good' and if they had nothing but positive experiences of others, their values would show themselves in their pure form. But what happens is that they start to develop beliefs in response to their experience of the world and people in it. Their beliefs then influence their intentions, commitments and ultimately what they do – their actions.

Gary's story

To illustrate how this works, consider Gary's story. Gary was in his late forties when I met him, and had spent most of his adult life in various prisons in the United States. His tall imposing stature was daunting enough but when I got closer I spotted his scar. It was deep and wide and wound its way almost all around his neck. I do not know how he got it, but from what he told me about life in prison I imagine he could as easily have got it there as outside.

Gary was brought up in an extended family of criminals. Most of them were drug addicts or alcoholics. He only ever knew a life of crime. 'To me it was you people who were wrong, weird, not living the right kind of life. It was you who had the problems,' he told me. He was in a gang that fought other gangs because of their different racial origin. The gangs existed in prison too, again organised along racial lines. The violence was extreme. It was normal. Inter-gang murders were common. This was Gary's life. It was all he knew. He told me that he trusted no one, cared for no one other than himself, not even his family. He told me he had no idea of what a different life could be, he did not know about how to treat other people decently.

Gary was not born a bad person but he quickly learned some defining beliefs that resulted in him becoming the archetypal criminal. He learned that no one was to be trusted, that the way to be successful was to gain respect from your gang by breaking the law and being violent. He also learned that you were ultimately alone in life: no one would look out for you, you had to look out for yourself. There was no point in becoming attached to anyone as they would probably harm you in some way. He learned that you had to kick against authority and that the way to get anyone to look up to you was to be a 'hard man'.

With a set of beliefs like that, Gary inevitably aimed to 'screw someone over before they did it to me'. His intentions towards others were certainly not good or altruistic. The only commitments that he made were to himself or more powerful gang members, and they consisted of promises to either steal for drug money or hurt members of other gangs as a way of proving his power and increasing his standing in his gang.

The actions that Gary displayed were aggressive, threatening and violent.

When I met Gary he treated me with respect. He was polite and courteous. He told me how he had learned to do this. In his mid-thirties he faced yet another long prison sentence, but was given the option of joining a different kind of programme for prisoners. He chose the latter, where he essentially went through the kind of socialisation that a child undergoes. As he put it, he 'learned how to be decent'. He told me what was important to him in his life now. He talked about being able to give something to others, to feel a sense of achievement and satisfaction with his new life, to be able to teach others what he knew and to feel that people looked up to him because he did good things not bad ones. Because Gary had to learn ways to survive in his environment as a young child, his behaviour became governed by that need to survive. No one would ever have thought of him as a trusting or trustworthy person. The Gary that I met I believe is both. His values are evident and he has discarded the beliefs that had previously driven his violent and criminal behaviour.

Most of us do not encounter people like Gary in our everyday lives. However we certainly do come across people who have taken on beliefs that lead them to behave in a way that we do not trust. Think of a bullying executive. Perhaps that ogre was bullied as a child and took on the belief that you have to get power over someone else and show yourself to be tough or they might bully you. As with Gary, their belief becomes more established; they are not even aware of the fact that they have essentially created that reality for themselves. They live their lives acting as if their beliefs are true. They usually hold to them irrespective of the context that they find themselves in or the people that they are with. So is that to say that such executives cannot be trusted? Well, you probably would not trust them, but if they were able to become aware of those old beliefs and discard them, then they might well start to act in a way that you could trust. The challenge is their lack of awareness of their beliefs. Once that awareness comes, as it did with Gary when he met people who actually wanted to help him and stuck by him, there is a chance of discarding the old beliefs and taking on more useful ones.

With people who hold beliefs that result in them becoming untrusting, it is difficult to measure their trustworthiness or even their potential for trustworthiness. Most people that we encounter have not had to take on such beliefs to enable them to survive emotionally and psychologically. Most have some sense of what their values are, values that give us clues as to whether we can trust them. Their intentions, commitments, behaviour and actions are the ultimate test. The driving force, though, is their values – and it is easier to see people's actions than it is to see their values.

So how do we know whether we can trust someone? We can never really know. The only person we can really ever know about is ourselves. Let's look at us first.

Knowing me, knowing you

In *The Book of Yo!* author Simon Woodroffe tells the story of how he founded his restaurant chain Yo! Sushi. He also tells 'Simon's story':

> I got divorced in my late thirties and it threw me to my knees. For the first time I thought to myself that maybe a few, just a few, of my problems are of my own making, and nothing to do with other people or circumstances. Sounds trite, but it was a great realisation for me because I could start looking at my part in every single situation. I'd always had friends who visited the Alcoholics Anonymous programme and, although I didn't qualify for membership, I'd been to observe some of their meetings and was impressed. I learned that by listening carefully I could understand much better what was going on with others and myself.

MEASURING TRUST

Do you trust yourself?

Have you ever thought about whether you trust yourself? It seems an odd question and one that most of us have probably never considered. Yet knowing the answer gives us clues as to whether people trust us and how easily we tend to trust others. Consider the following:

1. Does a friend or business acquaintance have to earn your trust?
2. Do you mistrust people until they prove you can trust them?

3. If you have a 'gut feeling' about something or someone, do you tend to ignore it?
4. Do you need to be in control of yourself and what you do?
5. Do you need to be in control of your surroundings?
6. Do you mind being the odd-one-out or having a different opinion to others?
7. Do you avoid doing things that you find challenging, telling yourself, 'I can't do that'?
8. When someone accuses you of something, is your first reaction to feel guilty even if you are not?
9. Do you immediately feel defensive when someone criticises you?
10. Do you prefer friends for their objective merits rather than how you intuitively feel for them?
11. If someone puts forward a different point of view to your own, do you tend to assume that they are right?

Answering mostly 'yes' to these questions may indicate that you don't trust yourself as much as you could. If we are self-aware, confident in the kind of person we are, and sure about what is important to us, then we tend to trust ourselves. We are not talking about the sort of false confidence that Gary displayed when he was living his criminal life. Gary's was a bravado that he needed to keep himself psychologically, emotionally and, often, physically safe. Self-trust is realistic. It gives us the ability to trust our own judgement, to be inner-directed. It also gives us a sense of our own abilities, our strengths and talents, and also our weaknesses.

> People who do not trust themselves tend not to trust others. What is more, other people may find it difficult to have confidence in them. Why should we trust those who do not trust themselves?

Until recently, I always felt myself to be rather a coward when it came to adventure sports. Whenever I had tried them I hadn't been very good, and I had usually not enjoyed them because I was frightened. This bothered me as I am a person who likes to try new things and hates fear stopping me doing anything, and yet when it came to adventure sport I avoided even trying. I felt I was missing out so I decided to try and do something about it. I enrolled on a course in Wales. It involved abseiling, traversing a small canyon on a rope, rock climbing and jumping into the sea from a cliff. The thought of doing all of these activities terrified me. I felt very stressed in the weeks preceding the course and when the day came I felt sick with anxiety.

The course leader, a man called Dave, was one of those people who instils confidence. He came across as competent and quietly confident, and acted as though these were the kind of things that people did every day – they probably did! I immediately trusted him and felt as though I would be safe in his hands. In fact, I trusted him far more than I trusted myself in this particular situation. If he said it was possible and I could do it, then I thought I probably could. I realised later that because I trusted him in this situation and I did not trust myself, I actually handed over the responsibility for my safety over to him.

Several hours and many nerve-racking moments later, I had completed all the activities. I imagine that Dave comes across people like me regularly. He is an expert and I am an amateur, so it is understandable that I would put myself in his hands. However, the experience made me consider whether there are other times in my life when I do not trust myself to do something or to do it well.

Do others trust you?

Trusting ourselves is key if we are to be trusted and to trust others. However, it is not the only factor. The other important part of the equation is to do with our integrity and how much other people feel that we can be relied upon to treat them with respect. It is about whether we can keep confidences, whether we show consideration for others' feelings and opinions and whether our intentions to others are good. All these factors are important determinants of whether others trust you.

How can you gauge others' trust in you? Ask yourself whether, in general terms, others tend to trust you. You will probably be able to come up with the answer if you are honest with yourself. If we think about the people we work with, we can probably go through the list and quickly say which ones we think trust us, which do not and which we are not sure of. If we have any on our list that we think do not trust us then we can probably say why. Of course, this exercise takes honesty and a certain degree of self-awareness. Most people have a good idea why those that trust them do and why those that don't, don't. Reasons for the latter usually include things like people not sharing information with me freely, being cagey when I ask them questions, seeming to edit the information they give me and relating to me on a superficial level.

> Trust is an 'either/or' – and I'm not normally an 'either/or' man. It exists or it doesn't. I start by trusting people, once it's abused I never give it back.
> (Arie de Geus)

Do you think people usually trust you? If you are not sure or are interested in discovering the level of trust that people may have, consider the following questions:

1. Do people tend to open up to you and tell you things about themselves that they do not tell many others?
2. Are you generally accepting and non-judgmental of others?
3. Do people freely offer you help and support?
4. Do people come and seek your advice?
5. Do people feel comfortable being vulnerable around you?
6. Do you readily admit when you are wrong or have made a mistake?
7. Do you tend to use sarcasm and make put-down comments about people?
8. Do you gossip about others more than just occasionally?
9. Do you tell lies if it will benefit you to do so?
10. Do you like to make yourself look good even if it is at the expense of others?
11. Do you take credit for things that others have done?

If you have answered 'yes' to questions number 1 to 6 and 'no' to questions 7 to 11, then there is a good chance that people trust you.

It is very difficult to fake trustworthiness. If you are a trustworthy person, the chances are that it comes naturally. Your values and beliefs are aligned so that trusting others and being trustworthy are natural ways of being. We saw from Gary's story that it is possible to realign your beliefs. It is not easy though. Trust tends to be something that people either feel for you or they do not.

If we are to develop trust, people need to experience consistent behaviour. One small betrayal can destroy it and it can be very difficult to recover.

Can you increase your trustworthiness?

If you scored low on trustworthiness in the last questionnaire, you can work on changing the way you behave toward people to develop their trust. However, that will only work if you are doing it because you want to improve the quality of your relationships and connection with people *for the sake of those relationships and connections.* If you want to improve them for some kind of personal gain then it simply will not work.

If you want to increase your trustworthiness for its own sake and not for personal gain or to manipulate someone, here are some actions that will help:

- Communicate with the intention of relating, not of controlling or manipulating.
- Be open and genuine.
- If you are feeling or acting critical or judgmental, check your impulse.
- Try to understand other people's intentions; do not judge them just on their actions.
- Show genuine interest in people.

- If you are not interested in someone, do not try and fake it (they will know).
- Be honest, do not lie.
- Give others a chance to have their say and genuinely listen to them.
- Be open minded.
- Do not blame; try to understand instead.
- Admit to your mistakes and say when you are wrong.
- Apologise when necessary.
- Do not get defensive.
- Follow through on your commitments and do what you say you will do.

If these behaviours do not come naturally, however, it is hard to acquire them. You have to want to improve your relationships with people for the sake of those relationships. If that is not your aim then do not try this; they will trust you less because they will assume that you are 'being nice' as a way of manipulating them.

11 Attitudes to trust

It is worth recalling the events of 1962, when John F. Kennedy sent former Secretary of State, Dean Acheson, to brief Charles de Gaulle about the Soviet deployment of nuclear missiles in Cuba. Acheson offered de Gaulle a full intelligence briefing, but the French President told him it wasn't necessary, saying he trusted Kennedy never to risk war unless he was sure of his facts. After the diplomatic debacle over Iraq, it is hard to imagine a similar level of trust today.

(James P. Rubin, US Assistant Secretary of State for Public Affairs, 1997–2000)[1]

What matters is not simply how much we know, but how we react to what we do *not* know. This is essential if trust is to be developed, but what else is needed for it to take hold and thrive? How should we behave if we want to create trust? This chapter answers these questions and provides valuable insights from our *Trust Survey*.

UNDERSTANDING TRUST

What is at the core of trust? What are the values that we need to understand and aspire to if we are to be recognised as trustworthy? As with much about trust, these deceptively simple questions are intriguing and revealing to answer. During 2003, we undertook an international survey of people's attitudes to trust and gained a unique snapshot of people's feelings about this issue.[2] The survey was intended to help us understand more about people's attitudes to trust around the world and in different types of organisation, in particular:

- who people trust and why
- who people do not trust and why
- what trust means to people, and their experiences of it
- what people look for when deciding to trust someone – and what they find
- when trust is most valuable.

Issues raised by the survey certainly merit further investigation and verification, but our findings were very illuminating. We asked people to rate the significance of a wide range of attributes when deciding whether to trust someone. The ten most frequently reported were:

1. Fairness.
2. Dependability.
3. Respect.
4. Openness.
5. Courage.
6. Unselfishness.
7. Competence.
8. Supportiveness.
9. Empathy.
10. Compassion.

We call these the *drivers of trust*. Understanding and delivering each of these qualities is vital if trust is to be developed. These attributes are typically what we look for when deciding whether to trust and, quite probably, how much to trust someone. However, the reality of trust, meaning the attributes that we normally find, is quite different from this list. When we asked people which attributes were most frequently encountered, we found the following results:

1. Likeability.
2. Dependability.
3. Critical.
4. Ambition.
5. Fairness.
6. Professionalism.
7. Competence.
8. Respect.
9. Controlling behaviour.
10. Predictability.

We call these attributes *the reality of trust*. Interestingly, only four of these – fairness, dependability, respect and competence – were in the top ten drivers of trust. In other words, six attributes that we value significantly are relatively scarce: openness, courage, unselfishness, supportiveness, empathy and compassion.

We then looked a little deeper at the responses. We had asked people two questions:

- Rate the significance of these attributes when you are deciding whether to trust someone, on a scale where 1 is unimportant and 5 is extremely important.
- How often are these attributes found (1 is never and 5 is always)?

By subtracting the average scores for the second question from the average scores for the first, we were able to identify those areas where what we find in reality falls short of what we look for, our ideal. We call this variance *the trust deficit*: a gap in our expectations. The attributes with the biggest gap between what we want and what we find are:

1. Courage.
2. Unselfishness.
3. Fairness.
4. Openness.
5. Compassion.
6. Respect.
7. Dependability.
8. Empathy.
9. Visionary qualities.
10. Supportiveness.

No less than nine of these attributes are in our top ten most sought after (all except visionary qualities). So, to develop trust we should understand what these attributes mean for the way we relate to people. Remember, not only are these the qualities that we typically look for when deciding whether to trust someone, they are also the qualities where our expectations are most seriously missed.

BRIDGING THE TRUST GAP

Trust is recognised as being fragile and tricky to build, so it should come as no surprise if this list appears demanding, perhaps even daunting. To succeed, it is worth taking the time to consider each attribute in turn, finding a personal meaning that you understand, value and aspire to. Our perceptions on each issue are described below to start the process.

Be courageous

This means different things to different people but, above all, it implies an ability to do and say what you mean, especially when faced with adversity. It also requires a capacity to take risks, to be constant and determined, to admit mistakes and to stand alone when necessary. The value of courage is that it is universally respected, so, even if we do not agree with a particular idea or approach, we admire bravery and associated qualities of integrity, conviction and determination. Moral courage – the courage of our convictions – is present in those people that we choose to trust.

An example of moral courage is provided by SABMiller, who at the time of writing are the world's second largest brewer. During the apartheid era in South Africa, they were a strong regional business, but with the end of the white regime came a rapid rise to global prominence. The firm's courage is displayed in two notable ways. First, its policy makers decided that despite SABMiller's origins they would move it from being a strong national and regional player, to being a global brewing business. No small decision in such a competitive and established industry. This in turn led the firm to rely on its ingenuity and initiative.

The firm (formerly known as South African Breweries) had never been a favourite of the apartheid regime – despite its economic significance – as the leaders of the government had personally invested in the wine industry and were not keen on brewing. This led to some distance between SAB and the government, with the effect that they were always pushing at the boundaries of what was possible. In particular, senior executives recognised the disadvantages of a situation where so many of their workforce were poorly educated, distracted and demotivated by the problems of living in an oppressive state. Hence, SABMiller's code of employment reinforces the principles of enlightened and humane employment practices by eliminating discrimination, promoting training and development skills and by recognising employees' inalienable right to organise and negotiate their conditions of employment. This did not simply materialise when apartheid ended; it started during the apartheid years – despite obvious governmental pressures – because it was right and provided the only sensible future. Graham McKay, SABMiller's chief executive, comments: 'As South Africans we weren't really frightened of emerging markets, compared to the things that we were going through at home.'

With the demise of apartheid and their decision to take the opportunity to compete globally came many complications, and one of these was the need to improve their manufacturing processes rapidly and comprehensively. To achieve this, SABMiller took their production staff out of the business for two years while they improved their standards of education. The firm then felt able to implement the world class manufacturing initiatives that gave the firm a sound foundation in the 1990s.

Steve Carter, a consultant with significant experience of SABMiller, highlights the value of a 'protective frame' in enabling managers to find their courage.[3] This comes from an ability to choose how to engage with a situation. With SABMiller, the safety frame comes in two forms. First, there is an acceptance that they conquered their own domestic market decades ago, which leads to a belief in their principles together with an understanding of what it takes to sustain and extend this success into the future. Second, they have the confidence that comes from their work environment, where people, their ideas and enthusiasm are valued.

Behave unselfishly

One of the biggest counters to trust is a feeling that people are motivated by narrow self-interest, that life (and particularly commerce) is a zero-sum game. If this view predominates then logic dictates that the only sensible course of action is to always put oneself first. However, there are two problems with this view. First, life is not simply a zero-sum game with winners and losers; it is much more complex (and interesting) than that. Second, even if it were a win–lose game, and there are certainly occasions when someone must 'win' at another's expense, behaving selfishly is not always the answer.

If the idea that to build trust we should act unselfishly seems disconcerting or even naïve, do not worry. People understand when others need to act for themselves, and this does not necessarily jeopardise trust. Selfishness means more than acting in your own best interest: it implies 'doing others down' for narrow personal gain – and it is this that is to be avoided.

However, of even greater significance is recent scientific research suggesting that trusting is a natural human phenomenon. According to recent evidence, we may be instinctively predisposed or 'wired' to trust others.

When it comes to understanding trust and its relationship with selfishness, conventional logic is dominated by the Nash equilibrium, which predicts that in economic transactions between strangers, where one has to make decisions based on a forecast of another's response, the optimal level of trust is zero. To illustrate this point, consider the example of a game where Player 1 has to decide whether to send Player 2 some of his or her $100 stake. If the money is sent, it will be tripled and the anonymous partner can choose to return none, some or all of the cash. Two questions dominate: why should Player 2 send anything back? And why should Player 1 give anything in the first place? The Nash equilibrium says it is better for Player 1 simply to retain the stake and do nothing. However, despite this economic orthodoxy, over the course of hundreds of tests, the Nash Equilibrium is disproved. In reality, about half of Player 1s send some money, and three-quarters of Player 2s who receive it send some back. According to Paul Zak of Claremont Graduate University in California, who leads the team doing these experiments, 'the reason that this high degree of trust in the laboratory is proving a

> 'Experiments are now confirming what life teaches us: people frequently choose to be cooperative, trusting and generous during economic negotiations. This is because it is in our nature to trust.'
> (*New Scientist*)

mystery to economists is that they haven't taken into account the neurological component of trust'.[4]

Zak explains that our brains have been tailored by evolution to cope with group living. So, along with our Machiavellian intelligence – which allows us to outwit rivals for mates, food and status – our social brain is also adapted to be cooperative. Individuals can benefit by working together. But that requires trust, which is why, according to Zak, we have a biological urge to trust one another.[5] In fact, these ideas are gaining ground even in traditionally 'hard-edged' disciplines with the development of the relatively new field of neuroeconomics, which aims to understand human social interactions through every level from synapse to society. Neuroeconomists believe that their findings about the nature of trust will provide the potential to help make societies more productive and successful. According to the 2002 Nobel laureate and neuroeconomist Vernon Smith of George Mason University in Virginia:

> As we learn more about the remarkable internal order of the mind, we will also understand far more deeply the social mind and therefore the external order of personal exchange, and the extended order of exchange through markets. We are just at the beginning of a great intellectual adventure.

Recent research has focused on finding the biological mechanisms that underpin trusting behaviour, and one promising approach has been to correlate variations in trust with changes in the levels of eight hormones. Only one has emerged as a strong candidate for a human 'trust chemical': oxytocin, a reproductive hormone. Studies in animals also link oxytocin with pro-social behaviours such as bonding with offspring and with sexual pair bonding in some mammals. Now researchers are taking these findings one step further to show how oxytocin might underpin behaviours such as trust in humans. Oxytocin production is triggered by pleasant experiences, including eating and sex. The hormone acts in parts of the brain (such as the limbic system, notably the amygdala and the pre-frontal cortex) associated with the emotions, memory and decision making; all are essential for social interactions and significant for trust.

It seems that oxytocin production may be triggered naturally when someone shows trust in us, in much the same way as adrenaline production is triggered naturally when we are faced with danger (the 'flight or fight' response). In this case, the urge to respond positively when someone shows trust is largely outside our control. Paul Zak's view is that:

> In light of the underlying neural anatomy, our experimental results suggest that oxytocin influences human trust decisions in ways largely beyond the realm of conscious perception, since the structures where it is activated are situated outside the large frontal cortex. Trust in our species therefore appears to be driven by an emotional 'sense' of what to do, rather than a conscious determination.

Value fairness

The next attribute we look for when deciding to trust is fairness. People who are most often and most easily trusted behave fairly. This means that they treat others:

- according to what is understood and accepted to be reasonable
- as they would wish to be treated themselves
- in a consistent, even-handed manner.

Being fair does not simply mean avoiding inequity and preventing unfairness; rather, it implies a dynamic, proactive desire to seek out what is just and then follow that course. In this respect, fairness links closely with the need to be courageous, unselfish, open, empathic, compassionate and consistent.

An example of a firm that recognises the importance of fairness is Canon, one of the world's largest makers of office equipment and computer peripherals, as well as consumer electronics and optical products. Fujio Mitarai, Canon's president and CEO, is credited with making the tough decisions that have allowed the company to thrive, despite its relatively mature core businesses. Mr Mitarai has combined traditional Japanese attention to product quality with the traditional American focus on the bottom line. Most significantly, he has been meticulously fair and has honoured another Japanese tradition, job security, by avoiding lay-offs, even if it has meant discarding product lines. This approach has resulted in a loyal and hard-working workforce – and the results speak for themselves (Table 11.1).

> **Our research highlighted an uncertainty about whether trust results in increased profits. Make no mistake, individuals and organisations that are characterised by courage, unselfishness, fairness, openness, compassion, respect, dependability, empathy, vision and supportiveness are trusted – and they prosper.**

Be open

'Try to be transparent, clear and truthful. Even when it is difficult and, above all, when it is difficult.'

This view from Jean-Cyril Spinetta, Chairman and Chief Executive of Air France, highlights the importance of openness and transparency for trusted leadership. Openness is most frequently discussed in relation to corporate

Table 11.1 Canon's financial performance, 1997–2001

	1997	1998	1999	2000	2001
Revenues (¥ bn)	2,761	2,826	2,531	2,696	2,908
Net earnings (¥ bn)	119	110	70	134	168
Earnings per share (¥)	135	124	80	152	189
Share price (ADR, US$, end of year)	23.35	21.50	40.56	33.69	35.06
Market value (¥ bn, end of year)	2,635	2,102	3,539	3,503	3,952
Return on shareholders' equity (%)	11.2	9.7	6.0	10.7	12.2

Source: Economist Intelligence Unit (www.eiu.com).[6]

governance issues, but it is no less important in the appearance and feeling one gives to others. Are you approachable? Do people feel inclined to come and talk to you?

An example of the significance of openness is provided by Federal Express, the first express delivery company to offer end-to-end tracking of the status of a package from pick-up to delivery. FedEx went on to ensure that information is made available on-line. Customers clearly value this level of openness and transparency and choose to trust firms offering this service. Today, many Internet retailers also provide positive tracking of customer orders and deliveries on-line, using the information services of their express delivery partners.

Openness matters because people who shift their viewpoints or are genuinely unclear about an issue are not easily trusted. Openness is therefore linked with one essential quality: self-awareness. This may seem counter-intuitive when it comes to the issue of trust, which is focused on other people and relationships. However, being self-aware is an important and frequently neglected issue. There are many psychometric diagnostic tools, such as Myers-Briggs, Enneagram and 16PF, specifically designed to help people understand their behaviour and motivation. While some of these tools may have inherent weaknesses and their efficacy is contentious, what is significant is that they highlight a need for greater self-awareness, and this is beneficial when building trust. So, what do we mean by self-awareness and how does it help openness?

> Openness matters, because people who shift their viewpoints or are genuinely unclear about an issue are not easily trusted.

What we do not mean is selfishness or acting out of self-interest. Self-aware people understand their own motivations and desires and the impact that they have on others. They tend to be more honest and open.

In discussion with executives and people replying to our trust survey, several principles emerged that can help develop and sustain openness, and lead to greater trust. First, *engage people*. When people are actively invited to participate in activities or decisions, then there is often (not necessarily always) a positive feeling that their contribution will be valued. Of course, simply inviting people to contribute may not be enough to engage them. Engagement means involving individuals in decisions, respecting their contribution and encouraging them to challenge each other. Incidentally, this approach is also likely to result in better ideas, to generate collective understanding and wisdom and to bring success – conditions in which trust is more likely to thrive.

Providing clarity and explanations about decisions is also important for openness and trust. It reassures people that their opinions have been considered and it opens up the reasoning and intention behind a decision.

A major advantage of openness is that it engages people – and for organisations, this includes customers as well as employees, suppliers and others. This need not be difficult or complex, but it is important to ensure that you are understood. The value of openness is highlighted by the example of Ryder, one of the largest truck-leasing businesses in the world. During the early 1990s, Ryder suffered a steady decline in their business. This was in common with the rest of their industry, which was suffering the effects of recession; however, in the market for truck rental by consumers and small businesses, Ryder slipped to second place. Their response included a range of significant measures, but chief among them was an understanding of the need to use information so that their business was more open to their customers.

The Ryder approach to openness highlighted three key influences from the customers' perspective:

1. The need to help customers buy: for example, by producing a brochure explicitly explaining why they should buy Ryder's insurance covering damage to the truck, as well as providing another brochure offering other supplies and accessories. Ryder also recognised that customers would want to compare them with their competitors, so they produced a truck comparison chart, highlighting their competitiveness and reassuring potential customers.
2. The need to help customers use the service: Ryder provided a free guide to moving (entitled *The Mover's Advantage*) to every customer and potential customer, published in Spanish and English.
3. The need to help customers continuously adapt their usage: as well as ensuring that each outlet was well-ordered, displaying a strong sense of corporate identity and commitment to customer service, Ryder also ensured that there were additional products and services available at their outlets. This included information about the advantages of towing

using Ryder's equipment, and details of longer-term discount rates to attract customers back.

The measures that Ryder adopted helped customers to buy through readily providing information, establishing openness and trust with them and providing peripheral clues as to the quality of the business. For instance, each outlet was inspected monthly (not quarterly, as before) to ensure that items such as literature, banners and signage were well laid out and appealing, enhancing the customers' perception of the business as well-organised and professional. These measures were among a range of actions taken by Ryder, and their overall approach helped to turn around their business during a time of recession, returning the company to the number one position in their industry.

Empathy, compassion and supportiveness

Although empathy, compassion and supportiveness are different attributes, they are closely related in the ways they contribute to trust. Consider empathy first. It can be defined as 'the power of understanding and imaginatively entering into another person's feelings'.[7] Compassion takes this further, and is 'a feeling of distress or pity for the suffering or misfortune of another'. Empathy and compassion are essentially about taking the time to understand the feelings of others, with compassion also recognising the need to do something about it. The reason people who display empathy and compassion are trusted is that they give others a sense that their feelings and circumstances are being considered and understood. In other words, there is more at play than simply the leader or decision maker's own self-interest.

> **Empathy, compassion and supportiveness can seem intensely personal attributes, yet what underpins them – making them relevant for firms and individuals alike – is *understanding* and a willingness to be flexible and helpful.**

Jean-Cyril Spinetta highlights the importance of empathy for generating trust and strong leadership. When asked what made someone a successful, trusted leader, he replied:

> First, value people. If you do not like people, do another job. Understanding, motivating, mobilising and communicating with people is essential, and this is especially true in a service business such as an airline. The leader needs to uncover people's talents ... but also be sure that people understand the strategy. If people are unhappy or angry then the company suffers.

When we asked people whom they trust most, Dell Computers scored unexpectedly highly. People commented that they like Dell because the staff understand and help them. It is as if Dell recognise that computers are complicated and expensive products, and understand that there is a real competitive advantage to showing genuine flexibility and helping people to buy.

Dell's strategy from their origins in the 1980s was to provide good quality personal computers at low (but not the lowest) prices, backed up with friendly and reliable after-sales service. They needed an aggressive strategy if they were going to compete against two formidable market leaders: IBM and Compaq. However, the real key to Dell's success was to carefully target their product offering by getting to know their customers in detail. Large amounts of advertising were placed in new (and unfashionable) magazines read by computer experts, raising the business's profile with this key group. Combined with this was Dell's direct-response advertising methods: in order to get the Dell product catalogue, customers either had to complete a detailed response card, or call a freephone number where they were asked the same, detailed questions. The Dell phone representatives were highly skilled, trained to ask questions but also to listen to customers, recording their preferences and requirements in detail and then acting on them. Potential customers were flattered at the interest and level of attention they were receiving and responded in droves, enabling Dell to amass an enormous database of vital information about each individual prospect and customer. This information was then used to help customers, tailoring product and service solutions to each individual need in a way that customers understood and appreciated.

The Trust Survey also confirmed the power of empathy, compassion and supportiveness, by showing whom we trust the *least*. Top of the list were dictators and politicians, distrusted by 51 per cent of people. People felt that these two groups lacked compassion, empathy and supportiveness. They did not take the time to understand 'real' people or issues, and are perceived as not placing any value on being supportive. There was a great wave of uncertainty about who came third, with people simply not knowing whom they trust least, reflecting the feeling that to distrust someone you need to know about their motives.

Respect

Trust is more likely to result when people are clearly shown respect, because that is seen as a clear, positive and engaging virtue. At times, showing respect can also be disarming and this, too, is positive for generating trust. When we asked our survey respondents whom they trust the most, the answers came back unavoidably intermingled with people they *respect* the most, as if the two words are interchangeable. Whether they are interchangeable or not is largely semantic. If people confuse respect and trust, and you want to build trust, then earning respect can be very important too. Some of the most trusted individuals mentioned to us were:

- Nelson Mandela
- George W. Bush
- Mahatma Gandhi
- Tony Blair
- Colin Powell
- Billy Graham.

(Interestingly, George W. Bush and Tony Blair polarised opinion, with an almost equal number of respondents viewing them as the *least* trusted politicians.)

Some of the most trusted organisations appear to include:

- Dell Computers
- BMW
- BBC
- Virgin
- Toyota
- UK National Health Service
- Mercedes
- Marks & Spencer
- Coca-Cola
- Amnesty International
- John Lewis Partnership.

It seems likely that the reason these people and organisations are trusted is that they are respected. They have shared values, providing a common language that brings people closer together. Trust occurs because people feel that these individuals and firms are on their 'wavelength', valuing what they value, seeing the world in a similar way and giving things the same relative importance as they do. This concept of *congruency* is a central pillar of trust and respect.

A common mistake made by individuals and organisations is to think that only a few people can be leaders and that trust and respect can only be the preserve of leaders. The humble origins and soaring principles of people like Gandhi and Mandela show that the need is not for trusted leaders, it is for trusted *leadership*. In other words, we all have a part to play and a contribution we can make. Trust and respect are qualities of the organisation as a whole, not just a facet of the few; everyone plays a part building and maintaining this.

What are the features of respected organisations? It seems that they have some (although probably not all) of the following valuable characteristics:

- clarity of vision and purpose
- a culture that recognises excellence and success
- energy and enthusiasm at all levels
- a clear process and ways of doing things, combined with …
- an openness to challenge and search for new ideas
- a belief among people that they have the power they need both to do their jobs and to contribute more widely to the organisation
- an emotional attachment among employees, with an expectation of reciprocal respect and support.

Above all, individuals understand how they will benefit, and are committed to others and to the organisation as a whole. In such an organisation, people will find the trust they need, whatever the situation. When a clear, compelling vision is needed, it is there. When people prefer solitude to get on and make a difference, it is allowed. When support is needed, it is available. Consequently, they deliver what they promise to their customers and stakeholders – and it is likely that this is why they are respected.

Leadership at any level is full of tough decisions; the way these are resolved has major consequences for the degree of respect that is accorded to the decision maker. There are many personal perspectives on building respect; however, respected people – like respected organisations – invariably possess some or all of the following characteristics:

- They know what it is that they have to achieve, possessing clarity of vision and purpose.
- They are interested in what they do, displaying energy and enthusiasm at all levels.
- They understand and accept the expectations that are held about them.
- They challenge and propose new ways of doing things, searching for new ideas.
- They feel they have the authority to take decisions, and exercise this authority responsibly.
- They are supportive, with an emotional attachment among colleagues and an expectation of reciprocal respect and support.

Dependability

There is an interesting exercise used to encourage people to trust each other. It involves one person standing about two or three feet in front of another and then, with closed eyes and a straight back, leaning back and toppling into the arms of the person behind. The one falling backwards has to depend on the other being ready and able to catch him or her. This builds and encourages trust by testing the catcher's *dependability*.

Interestingly, dependability is itself a self-sustaining cycle that perpetuates both itself and trust. This is because cooperation and collaboration are often integral to dependability, with people encouraged to support each other through practical help, good communication and in many other ways – from mentoring to sharing best practice and experience. Dependability also has something in common with the other attributes of trust, such as courage, unselfishness, fairness and compassion. Like them, it can mean giving up things – information, time, resources, pet projects – to help others succeed. To illustrate the impact of dependability, consider the three most trustworthy people you have ever met, and ask yourself: How dependable are they?

> Dependability is essential for trust. Without a concern for safety, reliability and support – the components of dependability – it is impossible for trust to exist.

Being dependable means being reliable and consistent. It enables people to understand what to expect and it facilitates communication and collaboration, as well as providing the certainty needed to encourage and motivate.

Corporate examples of dependability include such firms as Mercedes, BMW, Toyota, the BBC and British retailer Marks and Spencer, who all rated highly in our survey. A well-known example of corporate dependability is low-cost, low-fare Southwest Airlines, founded by Herb Kelleher, which shows that dependability does not mean being unimaginative or old-fashioned. It was the only US carrier to continue growing in the wake of the September 11 terrorist attacks and the only one to turn a profit in the first quarter of 2002. The airline, once serving the southwestern USA exclusively, continues to grow outside this region.

The firm's strategy is to provide quality air travel at low cost based on punctuality, and it consistently tops the rankings of airlines. Southwest was one of the first firms to make a virtue out of low-cost air travel; for example, by flying only 737s it was able to reduce maintenance and training costs. Its focus on simplicity and customer service has been a winning model in good times and bad: 2002 was the thirtieth consecutive profitable year in its 31-year history. This is even more striking in light of the global travel downturn after September 11. Its deep pockets enabled it to avoid lay-offs and to keep its schedule intact during the worst travel downturn in history. Many other firms, notably Ryanair and easyJet in Europe, have replicated its business model.

Southwest are not only dependable as far as their customers are concerned; they also have one of the most committed workforces in the country. In an industry renowned for regular labour disputes, Southwest has experienced just one strike. The firm has been among the top ten in *Fortune*'s 'Most Admired Companies' ranking for five years, and the company is Number 18 on the *Financial Times*' list of most respected companies worldwide.

Table 11.2 Southwest Airlines' financial performance, 1997–2001

	1997	1998	1999	2000	2001
Revenues (US$ m)	3,817	4,164	4,736	5,650	5,555
Net earnings (US$ m)	318	433	474	603	511
Earnings per share (US$)	0.41	0.55	0.59	0.76	0.63
Share price (US$, end of year)	7.30	10.88	10.75	22.35	18.48
Market value (US$ m, end of year)	5,604	8,646	8,642	17,798	14,916
Return on shareholders' equity (%)	15.8	18.1	16.7	17.5	14.9

Source: Economist Intelligence Unit (www.eiu.com).

Visionary qualities

If people are to place their trust in someone, they need to know where that person is heading (actually or metaphorically) and they need to be motivated to make the journey. If leaders are uncertain or lack the necessary motivation, then trust will be eroded. The value of visionary leadership, therefore, is that it provides a clear direction and set of values, and it motivates. Being visionary means encouraging people to look at activities in the long term, keeping in mind overall goals. The orientation is to the future, seeing things in the broadest context and appreciating broad principles. In a stronger form, it involves inspiring others with the goals to be achieved.

The ability to create and communicate an effective vision for their organisation or team is a real test of a leader's skill. This is what often defines successful leaders and sustains both them and their teams or organisations during good times and bad. People generally need to know where they are going, and what the overall purpose of their activity is: one of the reasons, therefore, that people need a leader is because they want to be inspired towards a positive vision of the future.

John Kotter, in his influential book *Leading Change*, identified a number of elements of a successful vision. In brief, these characteristics include:

> Developing a successful vision often means changing – or transforming – the organisation so that it can move in a determined way in the right direction. Vision and transformation are therefore closely interrelated in the same process of leadership.

- *Realism.* The vision must comprise feasible, attainable goals.
- *Power.* This has two parts: it must be *imaginable* and paint a clear picture

of what the future will look like; it must also *excite and inspire* as many people as possible.

- *Communicability.* It must be possible for the vision to be communicated to anyone, *quickly* (within a few minutes) and *easily* (without burying them in pie charts, reports, projections …).
- *Desirability.* The vision needs to appeal to the long-term interests of all the stakeholders; for a business these may chiefly include customers, employees and shareholders.
- *Focus.* The vision needs to be specific and 'real-world' enough to be used as a basis for strategic planning and to provide guidance for decision making.
- *Adaptability.* The vision needs to be general enough to allow individual initiative in how it is attained, and flexible enough to allow for changing conditions.

The process of developing and successfully realising a vision has several key elements.

1. *Developing the vision.* How this is achieved depends on the style of the leader and it may range from a consensus approach to a more directive style.
2. *Actively communicating the vision at all levels.* For the vision to have greatest value it needs to be shared and accepted, and while this may not be essential it is certainly desirable. Achieving agreement and unity around a common purpose is therefore a valuable aspect of leadership and will make progress to achieving the vision swifter and more likely.
3. *Using or implementing the vision.* To be fully effective the vision needs to routinely guide actions and plans across the organisation at all levels.
4. *Coping with problems and difficulties.* Clearly, the vision needs to be flexible and able to cope with changing circumstances. Given that the only constant is change, it will be fatally flawed and doomed to failure if it is too rigid or inflexible.
5. *Learning and adapting.* The leader needs to ensure that the organisation is fully prepared for the process of transformation and achieving the vision. This means not only developing people's skills, but developing their attitudes and approaches as well. What matters is not simply what people know, but how they react to what they do not know.

The history of politics is full of sparkling examples of visions that have inspired large numbers of people to great achievements. Martin Luther King's rallying call to Americans contained in his dramatic 'I have a dream' speech is one powerful example. So was Nelson Mandela's defence speech at his trial in the early 1960s. Consider these powerful words spoken by President Kennedy:

We choose to go the moon! We choose to go the moon in this decade and do the other things – not because they are easy, but because they are hard. Because that goal will serve to organise and measure the best of our abilities and skills, because that challenge is one that we are willing to accept, one we are unwilling to postpone, and one which we intend to win.

The reason these visions – and others – are so successful and inspire trust, affection and respect is because:

- They inspire and help people to get in touch with a greater purpose
- They tap into the needs of the audience, who positively *want* to be led.
- They are clear, simple and unequivocal. They don't ask, they tell.
- They generate confidence, not just in what is said but how it is said and the person saying it. This means that the vision must be credible – and that means coming from the right person at the right time.

A Fresh Perspective

Dr Kim Warren, Associate Professor of Strategic Management at London Business School and Chairman of Strategy Dynamics Solutions

Trust does not appear overnight. Rather, it builds up over time, like water in a bathtub. This notion is not limited to business and organisational contexts: building trust is a central mechanism of the human condition and the glue that holds our tribal species together. From the day a small child shares a toy with a friend, they start to understand the benefits of trust. They also start to see the limits of trust, and the opportunities to get what they want without it. If one falls out with a friend who fails to return a borrowed toy – well, there are plenty of other friends out there, so no matter. The more our societies have become dispersed and tribal groups fragmented, the less we rely on trust-based relationships and the less opportunity there has been for trust to maintain social cohesion.

Why does trust take time to build? Well, for us – as for a small child – no single incident on its own is enough to give us the confidence that we can trust a friend. Those who seem friendly might simply be being opportunistic, aiming to get what they want right now. However, every new occasion on which they show they can be trusted adds some water to the bathtub of the trust that we have in them. The more such incidents take place, and the more important they are, the more our confidence in them is increased. Think of this as nerve cells in the brain firing away to say 'trust this person' whenever you see them.

There are several further implications of this bathtub metaphor.

- *Trust is finite.* There is only so much water you can get in the bath (and only so many brain cells that can fire), so you cannot go beyond utterly trusting others.
- *Trust drains away unless constantly replenished.* We forget the favours others have done for us – and this leads to the third implication:
- *There is a limit to the number of people for whom we can find the time to make the gestures needed to maintain trust.* This is one reason why tribal communities rarely grow beyond 100–200 individuals, and why this size is often found to be a limit for truly effective organisational groups.
- *We can readily destroy trust.* Any time we let down someone who has previously trusted us, we throw some water out of the bathtub of trust that we have built up. Unless we are conscious that we are doing this, we risk being surprised to discover one day that someone we thought we could rely on does not support us as we expected. There is a minimum threshold of trust below which people's choices of action will switch away from helping us.

In our organisational lives, too, trust is stored up, or 'accumulated'. We trust as customers, employees, investors, business partners, subordinates, bosses or colleagues. These last three groups of trust relationships are closely equivalent to the interpersonal 'bathtubs' of trust that we build up in our general social relationships. We come to trust our colleagues, bosses and subordinates to make and fulfil reasonable commitments to us. Every time they do so, a spoonful of trust is added to our feelings about them. Any time they let us down, our bathtub of trust drops to a lower level, until eventually it falls below a threshold where we come to expect them to let us down and base our decisions and behaviours on that assumption.

Analogous processes take place with the banks, stores, airlines, on-line services and others with whom we interact as consumers. The more frequent and the more important our interactions with these providers, the more opportunities arise for them to fill up our stock of trust in them. Unfortunately, important and frequent interactions also raise the risk for them if they let us down. For these organisations, errors drain our trust bathtub quickly and seriously, until it drops to such a low level that it triggers us to take unfavourable behaviour: switching away from them to a competitor. In some cases, the difficulty or lack of opportunity to switch is so severe that we 'put up with' the situation, becoming resentful, trapped customers. Rail and air travellers and users of public services have all experienced the difficulties that this can cause.

Those who invest in us, too, build up trust and confidence in our ability to deliver the financial returns they expect. Each month that we hit our budget reinforces the feeling that their money is well invested and makes it less likely that they will switch to other investments. This situation illustrates a further feature of trust common to personal and business relationships: we can use a full bathtub to call in favours or ask for patience and tolerance. If we find ourselves in a difficult situation and unable to hit the commitments we have given, we can expect some degree of forgiveness for failure, especially if we warn those who trust us that we will on this occasion fall short of what they can usually expect of us. Finally, a solid trust relationship allows us to take shared risks with those who trust us. We can try out a new product with a key customer who knows us well, being quite open about the possibility that there may be teething problems.

For further exploration of these ideas visit www.strategydynamics.com for learning materials and further information, and www.strategydynamics solutions.com for coaching and training.

WHAT IS YOUR ATTITUDE TO TRUST

- *What does trust mean to you?* Where, when and why does it matter?
- *Whom do you respect and trust?* What is it about them that engenders trust? How do they benefit from this?
- *How could trust benefit your organisation?* In what areas would greater trust improve performance, for example, building your brand, strengthening customer loyalty, lowering recruitment costs, increasing innovation and enhancing leadership and productivity?
- *How much does your organisation lose because trust is weak or missing?*

In the final chapter, we highlight the basic laws of trust, the characteristics of trustworthy (and untrustworthy) managers, and what it means to trust and be trusted.

12 Final word: the basic laws of trust

This final chapter highlights the basic laws of trust, the characteristics of trustworthy (and untrustworthy) managers, and what it means to be trusted.

THE BASIC LAWS OF TRUST

Self-trust is a critical factor in creating trust

… and distrust is often a projection of absent self-trust. It is unlikely that others will trust you if you do not trust yourself.

Trust is an absolute

There is no such thing as partial trust: it is an 'either/or'. Either it exists or it does not. We either trust someone or we do not.

Waiting for people to prove their trust does not work

The issue is not 'can I trust them?' but 'I will trust them'. Trust is not only earned: it must be given. If you trust people, they usually live up to it.

Trust can take a long time to build and it can be destroyed in an instant

It can take much commitment, many actions and a long time to create trust – and only one small act to destroy it.

You cannot create trust if you view it as a means to an end

If you try to build trust cynically, you are unlikely to succeed. People who succeed in building trust: care about relationships; make and keep commitments, and value honesty and integrity.

You cannot create trust without respected values

The values of integrity and honesty are the basis of all trusting relationships and high-trust cultures.

Trust is often invisible

We often fail to realise that things are going well because of trust or going badly because of the lack of it. While trust is often invisible, it only exists as the result of constant actions and attention to the relationships and activities that create it. It is only when it disappears that we notice its absence. Its low profile does not diminish its power. In fact, trust often only becomes visible when it has been lost or abused in some way.

Trust requires commitment

Trust does not just happen. It requires commitment, personal responsibility and vigilance.

Trust relies on reciprocal relationships

Trust centres around the virtuous cycle of 'giving and getting' interactions. Well-balanced people get psychological satisfaction from being trusted, and, as they are trusted more, so their trustworthiness grows.

Trust opens up possibilities that can never exist without it

Without trust, people and organisations can never be totally efficient, creative and successful, because trust allows people to try new things, disagree with others and say what they want to say.

AND FINALLY

Remember trust is time-sensitive

We believe that trust is fundamentally important, potentially powerful and frequently neglected, but we also acknowledge that it takes time to develop. This brings its own complications. A firm that is trusted by its customers but despised by its employees may think the situation is fine. It is not. Trust and mistrust are like water: they flow, they get everywhere and they can be more powerful than they appear at first sight. Mistrust is especially corrosive so, for example, the firm will soon find that its problems with its workforce are inevitably being transmitted to its customers.

Understand your personal motivation and behaviour

People who have insight into their own behaviour and motivation can answer questions such as 'Why do I behave the way I do?' 'What motivates me?' 'What affects my behaviour?' Understanding these questions will enable you to deliver core requirements for trust, such as fairness, openness and courage. This personal insight is, of course, notoriously difficult to achieve, and many people make a great deal of money helping to find the answers.

Avoid the substitutes for trust

There is no substitute for trust. So avoid thinking that contracts and documents are a substitute for genuine trust. They may serve a purpose, but that is not creating trust; indeed, they can actually jeopardise it.

These principles help us to understand how we create, maintain or regain trust. However, we need to take several actions if we are to be regarded as trustworthy, and these are described in the next section. These principles build on the ideas explained in earlier chapters, and they start with the need to understand trust.

Avoid the power game

There is a tendency for people to prefer the pursuit of power to the pursuit of trust. It is easy to understand why: power is seen as providing control and security. It also feeds the ego. For some, this is paramount. They need power to feel good about themselves. Trust is much more durable, flexible and less brittle than power. It lasts, and it works better. Power implies a need to dominate and this is the antithesis of trust. In fact, the differences between power and trust are stark and sobering, and it is worth considering why trust works better than power.

If trust is so obviously significant and beneficial, then why is it so often destroyed and why do organisations overlook it and fail to maximise its benefits? The answer is often a preference for something that is easier, more certain and, for some, more satisfying: the pursuit of power.

> Exploiting power invariably stores problems for the future and misses opportunities in the present, whereas trust provides a firmer foundation for the future and more easily creates, recognises and maximises opportunities.

It is important to understand and value the benefits of trust. Once a person is identified as valuing and pursuing power, it can be hard to be seen as trustworthy. However, there are several challenges when promoting a trust-based approach in preference to a power-play approach. Trust takes time to build and develop, and this may not be a priority if time and other resources are limited. Trust may be seen as an expensive luxury, a distraction; or there may be cultural feelings that trusting means being 'soft' and vulnerable. Also, the other party may be insisting on playing the power game. To some people trust can imply uncertainty, whereas power in their view implies a more tangible, prescribed certainty. Finally, personal issues will be important: people who have benefited from trust tend to be more trusting, whereas those who have suffered from an abuse of trust tend to be less so.

Avoiding the power game means creating trust, and the benefits of the trust approach are stark and compelling when compared with the alternative.

Pursuing power means...	...whereas creating trust means:
Focusing on narrow self-interest.	Recognising that more is achieved and success is greater when people collaborate.
Creating fear.	Building understanding and valuing support.
Being autocratic, acting as if you are always right and know best.	Being consensual – going further with the help of others.
Dominating.	Being fair.
Communicating unilaterally.	Communicating bilaterally.
Maintaining flexibility ('wiggle room') for oneself while locking others into commitments.	Mutually agreeing commitments and flexibility.
Seeking mastery.	Valuing sympathy as well as mastery.
Avoiding dependence.	Creating interdependence.
Influencing through coercion.	Influencing through expertise, respect and understanding – and coercion where necessary.
Making arrangements and contracts that are closed, formal, detailed and prescriptive.	Pursuing open, associative, long-term relationships.
Reducing conflict through detailed prescription, constant monitoring and the threat of legal action.	Reducing conflict by working with people who have similar values, by increasing mutual understanding and resorting to mediation or arbitration to resolve disputes.

THE CHARACTERISTICS OF TRUST AT WORK

Characteristics of trustworthy individuals...	...and signs that they are untrustworthy
Always displays the highest standards of behaviour – and encourages this in others.	Often compromises personal integrity and ethical behaviour (for example, when placed under business pressure).
Builds and inspires the confidence of all stakeholders.	Seldom takes steps to build or maintain the trust of key stakeholders.
Acts as a role model for corporate values.	Sometimes contradicts colleagues and corporate values.
Behaviour is fair and consistent; ensures this underpins team's business conduct.	Sometimes behaves unreasonably, inconsistently or with a lack of respect.
Resolves issues positively and with integrity, encouraging trust between the business and stakeholders.	May sometimes undermine trust.

Do:

- Work on building trust only if it is genuinely important to you not because you are trying to gain something from it.
- Deliver what you say you will, and be true to your word.
- Act with integrity and sincerity.
- Treat others as you would wish to be treated.
- Understand those you are dealing with, taking time to find out how they work and what motivates them.

Do not:

- Focus solely on your own agenda.
- Believe that your boss is your only customer.
- Betray a confidence, or gossip.
- Be critical, cynical, negative or combative.

REMEMBER: TRUST IS NOT A COAT

Trust is not a coat we choose to wear when it suits us. Rather, it is a simple reliance on and confidence in the truth, worth, reliability and value of a person or thing. We may choose to trust different people at different times or in different circumstances, but we trust when we genuinely see evidence of truth and/or reliability. Some will try to get us to trust them because they are looking for a quid pro quo. Our research highlights that politicians are especially susceptible to this. When we asked respondents, 'Which current leader or public figure do you trust least?' over 80 per cent named politicians, notably George W. Bush, Tony Blair, Bill and Hillary Clinton. Similarly, when we asked respondents, 'Which is the least trustworthy name you can think of (organisation or person, living or dead, excluding religious figures)?' over 70 per cent answered with the names of politicians or political bodies, from Richard Nixon to the US Congress and the United Nations.

The problem is that if you explicitly ask people to trust you (and, realistically, the people who do this most regularly are democratic politicians), then people expect to be able to believe in the veracity, reliability and value of what they are being told and promised. If this is not delivered, then bitter disappointment and resentment ensues. The rare alternative to this is the politician who does not emphasise the need to be trusted but instead sets an example by simply getting on with what needs to be done, and then achieves success despite manifest obstacles. In this situation, people feel that their implicit trust has been vindicated; feelings of trust become so strong as to broaden into genuine affection and lasting respect. In the politics of the last century, it seems that only Nelson Mandela and Mahatma Gandhi fall into this category.

> Trust is not a coat, a temporary 'quick fix' approach that we can use when it suits us and discard when we choose. It is a genuine belief system. We do not trust people for our own gain. We trust them because it is the right thing to do.

A rare breed, but an example to us all – and especially to our political leaders. These two did not command public trust because they asked for it or even because they were successful. They commanded trust because it was a central aspect of their personalities. They believed in the essential elements of trust: the need to be fair, dependable, worthy of respect and giving of respect, open, courageous when necessary, unselfish, effective, supportive, empathic and compassionate. By displaying these values, they were able to motivate others, overcome obstacles and succeed. Neither was perfect, but both inspired the trust of others.

Appendix: Trust survey

SECTION 1: ATTITUDES TO TRUST

1. What percentage of your colleagues do you feel you can trust?

2. How important is trust at work? (1 = unimportant, 5 = essential)

3. Have you worked for an organisation where trust is explicitly (rather than implicitly) valued? (Yes / No)

4. What percentage of your time is spent on 'political' issues (such as building bridges with colleagues, helping others in the expectation that they will support you, ensuring you do not offend or upset people etc.)?

5. When you are pressured at work, are you more or less likely to trust someone?

SECTION 2: WHO WE TRUST

6. Which current leader or public figure do you trust most?

7. Which current leader or public figure do you trust least?

8. Which business organisation or brand do you trust most?

9. Which business organisation or brand do you trust least?

10. What is the most trustworthy name you can think of (organisation or person, living or dead, excluding religious figures)?

11. What is the least?

SECTION 3: WHY WE TRUST PEOPLE

12. a) Rate the significance of the following attributes when you are deciding whether to trust someone.

12. b) How often are the following attributes found?

Attribute	Importance when you are deciding whether to trust someone (1= unimportant, 5 = extremely important)	How often are these attributes found? (1 = never, 5 = always)
Ambition		
Compassion		
Competent		
Controlling		
Courage		
Critical		
Dependable		
Easy going		
Efficient		
Empathic		
Enthusiastic		
Fair		
Flexible		
Gentle		
Good communicator		
Independent		
Innovative		
Likeable		
Open		
Organised		
Popular		
Powerful		
Predictable		
Professional		
Purposeful		
Questioning		
Rebellious		
Respect		
Sceptical		
Self-reliant		
Sensible		
Sensitive		
Skilful		
Spontaneous		
Supportive		
Tough		
Unselfish		
Visionary		
OTHER (please name)		

13. To what extent does appearance and body language affect your decision to trust someone for the first time? (1 = never, 5 = always)

14. In your opinion, how significant is trust in the following activities?

Activity	Significant	Neither significant nor insignificant	Insignificant	Unsure
Building partnerships and joint ventures				
Leading and motivating people				
Negotiating				
Developing new ideas				
Sharing information				
Leading change				
Managing risk				
Increasing profitability				
Appointing personnel				
Selling				

SECTION 4: DEMOGRAPHICS

15. Where are you located?
    - Western Europe (excluding Scandinavia)
    - Scandinavia
    - Eastern Europe
    - North America
    - Asia-Pacific
    - Middle East/North Africa
    - Latin America
    - Sub-Saharan Africa

16. What is your job title?

17. What industry are you in?
    - Aerospace and defence
    - Agriculture
    - Automotive
    - Chemicals and textiles

- Construction and real estate
- Electronic and electrical equipment, household goods and products
- Engineering and machinery
- Financial services
- Food, beverages and tobacco
- Healthcare, pharmaceuticals and biotechnology
- Leisure, entertainment, media and publishing
- Mining, oil and gas
- Professional services
- Retailing
- Telecoms, software and computer services
- Travel, tourism and transport
- Utilities
- Not for profit sector
- Other (please specify)

18. How big is your company in terms of annual revenues?
    - Under $50m
    - $50m–100m
    - $100m–250m
    - $250m–500m
    - $500m–$1bn
    - Over $1bn

19. How many people does your organisation employ?
    - Under 50
    - 50–200
    - 200–1000
    - 1000–10,000
    - Over 10,000

Notes

Chapter 1

1. Robert Putnam, *Democracies in Flux: The Evolution of Social Capital in Society*, Oxford University Press, 2002.
2. Francis Fukuyama, *Trust: Human Nature and the Reconstitution of Social Order*, Touchstone, 1996.
3. Trust: How to Build It, Earn It – and Reestablish It When It's Broken, *Harvard Management Update*, September 2000.
4. Fons Trompenaars, *Riding The Waves of Culture*, Nicholas Brealey, 1997.

Chapter 2

1. *Hygiene Factors* are ideas that are so well codified and widely accepted as to become routine, embedded in an industry across all competitors. They result from the fact that organisations are always trying to discover ways of outsmarting the competition, and while not all ideas are equally effective, some are prominent and clearly successful. Initially, some organisations develop competitive advantage by exploiting these ideas, but over time others see the beneficial effects and will start to copy the same ideas, eventually becoming established as 'best in class'. Once an idea reaches this point it has become a hygiene factor, something that is generally recognised as a precondition for running any healthy organisation. The point about trust is that despite its value it can be disregarded by the need for a quick buck. The exception to this is certain industries where trust is an integral part of the product or service, such as the legal or medical professions.
2. Trust: How to Build It, Earn It – and Reestablish It When It's Broken, *Harvard Management Update*, September 2000.
3. Nirmalya Kumar, The Power of Trust in Manufacturer–Retailer Relationships, *Harvard Business Review*, November–December 1996.
4. Several quotations from Carlos Ghosn are reported by the Economist Intelligence Unit in their article CEO Agenda: Carlos Ghosn on Leadership, published on www.eiu.com, 29 October 2002.
5. This quotation appears in Stephen Carter and Jeremy Kourdi, *The Road to Audacity*, Palgrave Macmillan, 2003.

Chapter 3

1. The Trust Survey was a global research project conducted by the authors between July and September 2003. For a more detailed overview of the survey and its results, see Chapter 11, Attitudes to Trust.
2. This is according to a three-year research project undertaken at IMD business school by Professor Donald A. Marchand, involving over 1000 senior managers in 98 companies, across 26 industries and 28 countries. For further information see Donald A. Marchand, William J. Kettinger and John Rollins, *Making the Invisible Visible,* John Wiley, 2001.

Chapter 4

1. David Whyte, *The Heart Aroused*, Doubleday, 2002.
2. Fons Trompenaars, *Riding The Waves of Culture*, Nicholas Brealey, 1997.
3. Jim Collins, *Good to Great*, Random House, 2001.
4. Roger Harrison, *The Consultant's Journey*, McGraw-Hill, 1995.
5. Hock's comments are printed in Joseph Jaworski's *Synchronicity: The Inner Path of Leadership*, Berrett-Koehler, 1996.
6. Robert Galford and Anne Seibold Drapeau, The Enemies of Trust, *Harvard Business Review*, February.

Chapter 5

1. Jim Collins, *Good to Great*, Random House, 2001.
2. Ricardo Semler, *Maverick!* Arrow, 1994.
3. Julie Allan, Gerard Fairtlough and Barbara Heinzen, *The Power of the Tale: Using Narratives for Organisational Success*, John Wiley, 2002.

Chapter 6

1. David Whyte, *The Heart Aroused*, Currency, 2002.
2. Javier Bajer, *Innovation: A Way of Being*, Talent Foundation, 2001; www.talentfoundation.org.
3. Laurence Prusak and Don Cohen, How to Invest in Social Capital, *Harvard Business Review*, June 2001.
4. Tom Bentley, *Learning Beyond the Classroom: Education for a Changing World*, Routledge, 1998.

Chapter 8

1. Elisabeth Kubler-Ross, *Living with Death and Dying*, Macmillan, 1982.
2. David M. Noer, *Healing the Wounds: Overcoming the Trauma of Lay-offs and Revitalizing Downsized Organisations*, Jossey Bass, 1993.

Chapter 9

1. Jeffrey Pfeffer, *The Human Equation*, HBS, 1998.
2. Dale Zand, Trust and Managerial Problem Solving, *Administrative Science Quarterly*, June 1972, p. 229; and R. Wayne Boss, Trust and Managerial Problem Solving Revisited, *Group and Organizational Studies*, September 1978, p. 331.
3. R. Wayne Boss, Trust and Managerial Problem Solving Revisited, *Group and Organizational Studies*, September 1978, p. 338.

Chapter 10

1. Jo-Ellan Dimitrius and Mark Mazzarella, *Reading People: How to Understand People and Predict Their Behavior, Anytime, Anyplace*, Ballantine, 1999.

Chapter 11

1. James P. Rubin, Stumbling Into War, *Foreign Affairs*, September–October 2003. This comment contrasts the friendship and trust that has historically existed between the USA and France since 1945 with the bitter animosity that arose during 2003, following French opposition to the UN Security Council giving cover to an American-led invasion of Iraq.
2. During August and September 2003 we surveyed over 100 people, predominantly in Europe and North America, to gauge how people feel about the issue of trust. A copy of the survey questionnaire is provided in the appendix and the results are highlighted in this chapter and others.
3. The concept of a protective frame is explored in *The Road to Audacity* by Steve Carter and Jeremy Kourdi, Palgrave Macmillan, 2003.
4. To Trust is Human, *New Scientist*, volume 178, issue 2394, 10 May 2003, page 32.
5. Further information about the neurological aspects of trust are outlined in To Trust is Human; the quotations from Vernon Smith and Paul Zak are taken from this article.
6. Information provided by the Economist Intelligence Unit. For further details, see www.eiu.com.
7. Definitions are provided by *The Collins Dictionary and Thesaurus*, Collins, 1987.

Index